TO HELL AND BACK

TO HELL AND BACK

The banned account of Gallipoli by Sydney Loch

Includes a biography by Susanna de Vries and Jake de Vries

ISIS
LARGE PRINT
Oxford

Copyright © Susanna de Vries and Jake de Vries, 2007

First published in English in Sydney, Australia 2007
by
HarperCollins Publishers Australia Pty Limited

Published in Large Print 2008 by ISIS Publishing Ltd.,
7 Centremead, Osney Mead, Oxford OX2 0ES
by arrangement with
HarperCollins Publishers Australia Pty Limited

British Library Cataloguing in Publication Data
Loch, Sydney
    To hell and back: the banned account of
    Gallipoli. – Large print ed.
    1. Loch, Sydney
    2. World War, 1914–1918 – Campaigns – Turkey
    – Gallipoli Peninsula
    3. World War, 1914–1918 – Personal narratives,
    Australian
    4. Large type books
    I. Title II. De Vries, Susanna III. De Vries, Jake
    940.4'26

ISBN 978–0–7531–5689–6 (hb)
ISBN 978–0–7531–5690–2 (pb)

Printed and bound in Great Britain by
T. J. International Ltd., Padstow, Cornwall

This book is dedicated to Dame Elisabeth Murdoch, a great admirer of Sydney and Joice Loch. Dame Elisabeth's financial and psychological support during the long process of writing and editing Sydney Loch's life story and the account of his Gallipoli experiences has been invaluable.

To Hell and Back is also dedicated to the memory of the late Iain Loch, son of Sydney's brother Charles. For over a year we communicated with Iain by phone and e-mail. Although he became ill during that time, he was always helpful in providing vital information about Loch family history. Unfortunately, Iain Loch did not live long enough to see this book in print.

CONTENTS

INTRODUCTION

The Straits Impregnable — "the best book on Gallipoli" — banned by the censor

The first casualty when war comes is truth.
US SENATOR HIRAM JOHNSON, 1917

This is the point to which censorship has reduced us — that the German official accounts are far truer than our own.
C.E.W. BEAN, DIARY, 26 SEPTEMBER 1915

Strict military censorship was responsible for the withdrawal from bookshops of the second edition of Sydney Loch's *The Straits Impregnable*, a candid book about his war experiences described in a review at the time of its publication as the best written on Gallipoli.

While serving at Gallipoli, Sydney Loch, a former grazier from Gippsland, Victoria, had kept a detailed war journal, which he took with him when he was evacuated from Gallipoli on a hospital ship. Crippled by polyneuritis and wracked by typhoid fever, Sydney had been on the danger list in hospital at Alexandria, Egypt, before being shipped back to Melbourne. His long convalescence provided him with an opportunity to turn his war journal into a publishable narrative.

Unlike most narratives by Gallipoli veterans, the typescript of Sydney Loch's story was never submitted to military censors, as laid down in the wartime Rules for Censors, published in 1915.[1]

Sydney's literary agent, Harry Champion of Collins Street, Melbourne, put up half the money to publish Sydney's war journal. Champion considered it important that people sheltered from the grim reality of the Gallipoli campaign understood what the situation was really like.

To avoid censorship, the publisher proposed to call *The Straits Impregnable* a "novel" rather than a war memoir. He was aware that by publishing Sydney Loch's story as fact rather than fiction he could be prosecuted for contravening the War Precautions Act, which forbade distributing material likely to discourage men from enlisting in the Australian Imperial Force, which badly needed new recruits.

In July 1916, about half a year after the Anzacs had been evacuated from Gallipoli, the first edition of *The Straits Impregnable* was published in Melbourne under the author's pen name of "Sydney de Loghe". Although *The Straits Impregnable* was published as fiction, most of its readers would have perceived Sydney's vivid description of the horrendous conditions at Gallipoli as the truth, which had long been withheld from them by strict censorship. As a result, the book soon became a bestseller.

Sydney Loch's "novel" received excellent reviews in several papers. Miss Joice NanKivell, book reviewer for a Melbourne paper, regarded it as "the best book yet written on Gallipoli" and asked to meet the author.

The first edition of The Straits Impregnable sold out within a few months, so Harry Champion was keen to publish a second one. To drive home the point that the horrors observed in the first edition actually happened, and keen to do whatever he could to reduce the chances of the forthcoming conscription referendum succeeding, Champion rashly added a preliminary note to the second edition: "This book, written in Australia, Egypt and Gallipoli, is true." He placed the note facing the first page, where no reader could miss it. The second edition, with the note and a blue cover rather than the first edition's red one, was published towards the end of 1916.

The preliminary note in the second edition of The Straits Impregnable was brought to the attention of the military censor for Victoria, Major L. F. Armstrong. He demanded that the book be withdrawn from all bookshops and threatened Champion's small publishing house — and his author — with legal action for breaking the War Precautions Act. Major Armstrong was a former barrister, so Harry Champion asked his lawyer friend Maurice Blackburn to negotiate with the censor's office in an attempt to avoid prosecution.[2]

The lawyers proposed a compromise: under his pen name of "Sydney de Loghe", Sydney would write a series of newspaper articles about the danger Britain now faced and how those of British extraction should help defend it, and Harry Champion would publish

Sydney de Loghe's collected articles in a pamphlet at a later date.

By now it was apparent that the war in France was going very badly indeed. There were fears that German troops might defeat the Allies, and could even invade Britain. The awful prospect of a German invasion of Britain, the country where Sydney Loch's parents lived, is likely to have prompted him to accept the compromise proposed by the censor. To settle the matter without further complications, although by now he had very mixed feelings about war and the after-effects, Sydney wrote the required articles. In 1918, shortly before the armistice, Champion published them in a pamphlet under the title *One Crowded Hour, A Call to Arms*.[3]

The Australian novelist Miles Franklin, who had left America for London in October 1915, received a review copy of *The Straits Impregnable* from Harry Champion. As a friend of Harry's wife, she was entrusted with the secret that the author's real name was Sydney Loch and that he had served as a gunner and "brigade runner" at Gallipoli.

According to Miles Franklin and literary critic H. M. Green, *The Straits Impregnable* was "a work of literary merit", as well as the best account of the courage and endurance shown by the Anzacs, and a vividly written history of the Gallipoli campaign. Miles found the book "lively and amusing, with poetic descriptions of the landscape of Gallipoli".

Miles Franklin felt that Sydney's book should be published in Britain so the British would understand the psychology of the Anzac troops and the difficulties they had faced so bravely and without complaint during the Gallipoli campaign.[4] Consequently, she took steps to sell the British rights to The Straits Impregnable to Sir John Murray for his London publishing house. In the British edition, which was published in 1917, the note about the book being a true story was repeated. Although the war had just started to go very badly for the Allies, there is no indication that the British censor objected to the book. Through the publication of the British edition of the book, Sir John Murray and Sydney Loch began what was to be a long friendship. Later this friendship extended to Sydney's Queensland-born wife, journalist and author Joice NanKivell. Several of the Lochs' subsequent books, set in war-torn countries where the Lochs were working in refugee camps funded by the Society of Friends, would be published by Murray over the next two decades. During that time Sydney and Joice Loch would become two of the most remarkable members of the postwar generation, for their outstanding work with refugees.

The censorship provisions laid down in the Commonwealth government's War Precautions Act of 1914 (amended in 1915) were the equivalent of today's Official Secrets Act. At Gallipoli the War Precautions Act was strictly implemented, on orders from General Sir Ian Hamilton, Commander-in-Chief of the

Dardanelles campaign, and his subordinate, General Braithwaite.

The main purpose of strict censorship was (and still is) to prevent military information passing into the hands of the enemy. At Gallipoli, censorship was also intended to cover up the fact that the troops had only moved forward a few metres after that first memorable day in April 1915, when the Anzacs had performed almost superhuman feats in capturing some of the ridges and ravines above Anzac Cove.

To make certain that neither the public nor the enemy would learn about the terrible conditions at the front, all letters had to be censored. Each senior officer was personally responsible for censoring letters written by the men under his command.[5] Taboo topics included the high death toll, the unsanitary conditions in the trenches and the swarms of flies that settled on bloated corpses and then landed on the lips and food of the soldiers. "Multiple choice" postcards with non-committal phrases were issued and the troops were encouraged to use these when writing home.

The chief censor, Captain William Maxwell, censored all press reports that left Gallipoli. Any reports that revealed the darker side of the war were passed along the chain of command until they reached the elderly General Sir Ian Hamilton.[6] He then edited the press releases — and in some cases rewrote them completely.

General Hamilton was determined that the truth about what was happening on the Gallipoli Peninsula should not reach the press; the reputations and military careers of himself and his fellow generals were at stake. He was also, naturally enough, keen to hide his blunders. He wanted the press to publish stories that gave the impression that he was a brilliant leader and that, thanks to his leadership, the Turkish Army was on the verge of collapse.[7]

While it can never be proved that casualty figures for the Anzac landing were deliberately withheld from the Australian public, what cannot be denied is that the published numbers of dead and wounded on the first day of the landing were only a fraction of their real total.[8]

Private diaries and journals, kept by members of the armed forces, were also subject to the War Precautions Act. Even after troops had left Gallipoli, war journals intended for publication had to be submitted to the military censor's office. Censorship offices had been set up in each state capital in Australia, and *all* war articles had to be checked by them before they could be published.

Of course in 1915 it had been relatively easy to muzzle the press on the Gallipoli peninsula — in those days there were no mobile phones, emails or video cameras. The military censor's office controlled the one and only cable communication and the post office.

By June 1915, censorship had reached such a pitch that the experienced British war correspondent Ellis Ashmead-Bartlett claimed angrily that "censorship has passed beyond all reason . . . anything of interest cut out . . . only a few dry crumbs left for the (poor) wretched public".[9]

Keith (later Sir Keith) Murdoch, a former Melbourne journalist, visited Gallipoli in September 1915 on his way to London to work as manager of the cable service of the *Sun* and the Melbourne *Herald*. Reluctantly, General Hamilton, who distrusted all journalists, allowed Murdoch to make a four-day visit to Gallipoli to investigate the postal services for the troops, but Murdoch had to sign a form declaring that he would submit *everything* he wrote to the Army censors first.

Ellis Ashmead-Bartlett had become increasingly hostile towards the British leadership at Gallipoli and in particular towards General Hamilton, because he was convinced that landing troops on the "impregnable" peninsula had been a terrible mistake. Ashmead-Bartlett believed that a catastrophe was imminent unless the Prime Minister and the War Cabinet in London were told exactly what was going on. He believed that if they knew what was really happening they would withdraw all troops from the peninsula.

Ashmead-Bartlett wrote a long and well-reasoned letter, explaining the situation, and addressed it to British Prime Minister, Herbert Asquith. In the letter Ashmead-Bartlett recommended the immediate evacuation of troops to prevent more needless slaughter. In order to circumvent the censors, Keith Murdoch, now about to return to London, agreed to take Ashmead-Bartlett's letter with him and deliver it in person to the British Prime Minister.[10]

A rival journalist informed General Hamilton that Murdoch was carrying Ashmead-Bartlett's letter. When the young Australian journalist landed in Marseilles he was met by a British Army officer with an escort of soldiers and *gendarmes* — his options were to hand over the "whistleblowing" missive or be arrested.[11]

The confiscation of this important letter, and the fact that an Army officer threatened to arrest him, made Keith Murdoch so angry that he was prepared to defy the War Precautions Act. Arriving in London on 21 September 1915, Murdoch wrote what he could remember of Ashmead-Bartlett's account in a far more emotive letter. He was deeply concerned about the large number of young Australians killed at Gallipoli. He went so far as to describe the outcome of one battle as nothing short of "murder" by British generals. Murdoch addressed his letter to Australia's Prime Minister, Andrew Fisher, and for good measure sent a copy to British Prime Minister Herbert Asquith.

In London, Murdoch made contact with Lord Northcliffe, editor and proprietor of *The Times*. Lord Northcliffe introduced Murdoch to Lloyd George, soon to become Prime Minister, and other Cabinet ministers who had been against the Dardanelles campaign from the start. As a result, Murdoch's letter was taken very seriously indeed; it was even submitted to Cabinet.[12]

On 28 September, General Braithwaite had told Ellis Ashmead-Bartlett that his letter had been confiscated and ordered him to leave the peninsula immediately. Ashmead-Bartlett returned to London, where he and Guy Dawnay, a former member of Hamilton's staff, worked against General Hamilton. Ashmead-Bartlett's action and the damaging facts contained in Murdoch's

"Gallipoli letter" played a part in the recall of General Hamilton from his post of Commander-in-Chief (on 17 October 1915) and the decision to withdraw troops from Gallipoli and they left on 20 December 1915.

Murdoch's friendship with the powerful Lord Northcliffe prevented action being taken against him. He went on to a brilliant career as a newspaper magnate and philanthropist.

In 1916 Ellis Ashmead-Bartlett came to Australia on a lecture tour talking about his war experiences. Major L. F. Armstrong, Victoria's military censor, fearful as to what the former Gallipoli war correspondent might disclose in his lectures, demanded the complete text of all his speeches in advance. These demands led to angry arguments between the two men. Ashmead-Bartlett wrote in his diary that censorship was even worse in Australia than in Britain.[13]

The tragedy at Gallipoli was a crucible that turned Sydney Loch from an eager young soldier, who described himself as Colonel Johnston's "galloper" or message bearer, into a humanitarian author and aid worker who preferred rescuing war victims to waging war. Sydney later worked in refugee camps in Poland, Greece and Palestine and was decorated by the Polish, Greek and Romanian governments.

Sydney Loch's book *The Straits Impregnable*, named after the Dardanelles Straits of Gallipoli, forms the main part of *To Hell and Back*. We have supplemented his book with information about Sydney Loch's life, which we obtained from his unpublished autobiography, which is held in the manuscript collection of the National Library of Australia; from Joice Loch's writings; from photographs and letters held by Sydney's relatives; and from other sources.

Susanna and Jake de Vries

PROLOGUE

THE EARLY YEARS — PORTRAIT WITH BACKGROUND

Sydney Loch arrived in Melbourne at the age of twenty with a suitcase containing riding clothes, a dinner jacket and tails, his favourite books and a portable typewriter. Behind his abrupt decision to abandon plans to go to university and emigrate to Australia is the story of a shy teenage boy who adored Laura le Paturel, a beautiful and sophisticated girl five years his senior, who lived with the Loch family.

When he learned that the orphaned Laura was having a clandestine affair with his father, Sydney decided to go to Australia. He worked first as a jackaroo, and once he had learned about farming in Australia he became a sheep farmer, and combined this with writing.

Frederick Sydney Loch (always called by his second name) was born in London in 1889, the third son of Frederick Pharye and Georgina Loch. Sydney's father was a tall, distinguished-looking vain man with a small Van Dyke beard, which he grew to hide the large strawberry birthmark on his chin. The Lochs were

1

originally a Scottish family. A distant forebear, John Loch, was a wealthy director of the East India Company who later emigrated to Tasmania, where he became a successful grazier. Sydney's great-uncle, Sir Henry Brougham Loch, had been Governor of the state of Victoria, and on his appointment had taken the title of Baron Loch of Drylaw, the area near Edinburgh where the Lochs had come from.

Frederick Pharye Loch had been destined for a career in the legal profession and was articled to a London solicitor. However, he soon found that life in a lawyer's office bored him. Frederick had an excellent singing voice, and contrary to his parents' wishes, he left law to study singing at La Scala in Milan, Italy.

There Frederick moved in Bohemian circles. He wooed Georgina Burn, daughter of a London civil engineer, who had been sent there to finish her education and was studying singing and drama. When Georgina told her parents she was pregnant, they were outraged, and demanded that Frederick Loch "do the right thing" and marry her.

Georgina and Frederick were married quietly at the British Consulate and returned to London as Mr and Mrs Frederick Loch. The couple took a small apartment in the west London suburb of Ealing where Sydney and his two brothers were born and Sydney spent the first two years of his life.

Frederick never managed to obtain singing roles at Covent Garden and was forced to earn his living as a singing teacher, a fact that embittered him. Georgina was an excellent mother to her three sons, Charlie, Eric and Sydney, but raising and educating them on Frederick's meagre income was not easy.

Fortunately for the Loch family, Frederick inherited enough money from his father to buy a short lease on a three-storey house: 19 Upper Addison Gardens, Kensington. The Lochs' new home had a conservatory and a studio large enough to accommodate a grand piano. Frederick gave private singing lessons and flirted with young ladies whose affluent parents wanted their daughters to become proficient in what was known as "drawing room" music. Singing and playing the piano were desirable accomplishments for young ladies in this era — musical soirees were popular after-dinner entertainment among the educated classes. To inspire his pupils, Frederick often took them to Covent Garden Opera House to attend performances by Melba and other famous singers.

When Sydney was fourteen he became seriously ill with rheumatic fever. Fearing he might be left with a weak heart, his parents sent him to convalesce in a warmer climate. Granny Loch paid the fare for Sydney to travel to the French Riviera, where he spent six months convalescing with a childless aunt whose husband owned a villa at Nice.

His aunt adored her highly intelligent nephew. They took daily walks together around the old town, along boulevards fringed with palm trees and through Nice's colourful flower market. Sydney's schoolboy French improved markedly under his aunt's tuition.

When Sydney returned to London, bronzed by the sun and in good health again, he found one of

Frederick's pupils, Laura le Paturel, her widowed mother and her boisterous younger brother Arthur, installed on the top floor of the Addison Gardens house. The le Paturels, who had grown up in Jersey and spoke fluent French, were now living *en famille* with the Lochs. Mrs le Paturel's husband had died when his children were very young. His estate in Jersey had been sold, and the money had been put into trust for his son and daughter. As a result, Laura and Arthur would come into a modest inheritance when they turned twenty-one.

Mrs le Paturel came to London for an operation for breast cancer, after which she and her children stayed at the Lochs' residence. Unfortunately, the cancer spread. Laura delayed her debutante season and nursed her mother at home, aided by a series of professional nurses. A few years after her operation Mrs le Paturel died. Motherly Georgina felt sorry for the fragile and orphaned Laura and her brother and invited them to stay as paying guests.

Laura le Paturel was five years older than Sydney and was Frederick's most diligent and dedicated pupil. Her singing lessons were seen as providing her with an accomplishment rather than a career, although Laura herself wanted to become a professional opera singer. Her voice was pleasant, but it lacked the strength to fulfil her ambition. Besides, it was assumed that an attractive young woman with a private income would soon be married off (possibly even to one of the Loch brothers).

4

Sydney and Arthur le Paturel were close in age and became good friends. Arthur was very different from his elder sister — he was interested in sport and horses, and was looking forward to working for a while as a jackaroo in Australia. He had relatives who owned sheep properties and a stock and station agency in Melbourne.

Sydney's brothers attended Wellington, the exclusive private school, famous for producing Army officers. But Georgina did not want to send Sydney to Wellington — she was afraid he might get rheumatic fever again. Instead Sydney was enrolled in a local cramming establishment to study for a scholarship examination for Oxford. There he was supposed to read law, the profession his father had abandoned as a young man. But like his father, Sydney was not interested in law. He loved studying the classics and European history, had a good knowledge of Latin and a talent for languages. He hoped to become a professional author.

Laura encouraged Sydney to write seriously. She gave him books to read in English and French and bought him a second-hand typewriter. As Laura spoke excellent French, she also offered to improve Sydney's command of the language.

Laura took Sydney to London's National Gallery and showed him the great French paintings in the Wallace Collection. She had attended a finishing school in Paris and did her best to induce in Sydney a taste for the best in art, classical music and literature. Years later, in his unpublished autobiography, Sydney acknowledged his debt to Laura, saying that her friendship had "melted away the worst of my teenage uncouthness".

It was not long before Sydney was suffering the pangs and woes of love for Laura, despite the fact that she was older and more mature than he. Like most boys of that age, Sydney had problems expressing his emotions and was far too shy to tell Laura of his feelings.

When Sydney turned eighteen the lease expired on their Kensington house. As Frederick's supply of pupils was dwindling, he decided that the family should move away from London. Initially he considered moving back to Edinburgh, but he soon learned that there were already too many singing teachers in the cultural capital of Scotland. So the family decided to move to the provinces, where singing teachers were scarce and houses cheap to rent.

Mr and Mrs Frederick Loch rented Harker Lodge, a vacant Georgian mansion some 8 kilometres from Carlisle, in the county of Cumberland. Harker Lodge stood amid magnificent but overgrown grounds and had a tennis court, a stable block, large greenhouses and a conservatory. Carlisle and the much larger city of Newcastle upon Tyne were close enough and big enough for Frederick to find pupils and travel by train to teach them once a week.

Laura and Arthur le Paturel continued to live with the Loch family at Harker Lodge. Due to the remoteness of their new residence, the Lochs needed a car. Laura, who was now twenty-three and had come into her inheritance two years earlier, bought not one but two cars — a small one for herself and a large Rover for the use of the Loch family.

Laura taught Sydney to drive, which he enjoyed, as it meant spending time with the girl he loved. They also used to go horse-riding together on the afternoons when Sydney was not at his new cramming establishment in Carlisle, studying Latin, Greek and English literature. Laura paid for the upkeep of the horses. She also spent a great deal of her money on employing an elderly cleaning lady and a man, Birkett, to service the cars and tend the large garden.

Sydney's mother cooked all the meals and ran the rambling Georgian mansion with the help of the cleaning lady. Assisted by Birkett, she restored the luxuriant garden and greenhouses to their former splendour. Once a month a musical soiree was held at Harker Lodge, at which Frederick's pupils performed; Georgina would prepare candlelight suppers for them.

Whenever Frederick Loch went fishing in the trout stream near Harker Lodge, Laura would take a book and sit on the banks of the stream and read, perfectly happy to be with him. Each week, when Frederick travelled to Newcastle by train to visit his pupils, Laura would take him in her small car to Carlisle Station and pick him up again on his return.

It was still Laura's ambition to sing at Covent Garden, so Frederick, as her coach, accompanied her to London for first nights at the opera, and they would stay in a London hotel overnight. Ever trusting,

Georgina remained at home and tended her beloved garden.

Many years later Sydney described ruefully how: "At the time I failed to grasp that Laura was drowning in the golden waters of love for my forty-nine-year-old father."[1] Looking back on his adolescence, Sydney realised that Laura had been squandering her inherited money on the Loch family, and particularly on Frederick. It was Laura's money that had allowed Frederick to live like the squire of Harker Lodge.

As planned, Arthur le Paturel sailed to Melbourne at the age of nineteen. After having spent some time working as a jackaroo on a cattle property, his relatives employed him in their stock and station agency. Before he left, Arthur had urged the Loch brothers to join him in Australia, the land of opportunity. Sydney's elder brother Charlie, who had studied mining engineering in London, was the first to take Arthur's advice. After he married the daughter of Canon Deeds of Coventry Cathedral, the newlyweds sailed for Australia, the country that to the young Lochs represented freedom, excitement and a chance to make their fortune.

Arthur sent Sydney a bound volume of the poetry of Adam Lindsay Gordon as a Christmas present — it was full of poems that praised Australia's wide, open spaces, gum trees, blue skies and sunshine. Sydney vowed that one day he too would go to this sunny land of opportunity . . . and he would take Laura with him.

★   ★   ★

Laura never fulfilled her ambition to sing at Covent Garden. A family friend, who acted as her guardian, wanted her to return to London and make a suitable match, in the style of a Henry James heroine. These were the days of arranged marriages, and Laura's guardian proposed to introduce her to the younger son of a peer. This was also a time when many impoverished aristocrats were searching for heiresses to marry, but Laura's fortune was not considered large enough to support the heir to a grand title with a stately home or castle. Laura took one look at the photograph her well-meaning friend had sent and replied that she had no wish to be married off to *anyone*. She said she was far too busy with her singing lessons to leave Harker Lodge.

Laura organised a piano recital on the night of Sydney's twentieth birthday, to celebrate the occasion. Sydney never forgot how beautiful she looked that night, with her long golden hair ornamented with a single rose. Later he would realise that the words of the song she sang were prophetic:

> Plaisirs d'amour ne dure qu'un jour
> Chagrins d'amour dure toute la vie.
> (The pleasures of love are brief,
> The sorrows of love endure for life.)

After the recital there was champagne and birthday cake. The other guests departed and Laura and Sydney were left alone in the dining room. Sydney, unused to the effects of too much champagne, chose this moment to blurt out that he had always loved Laura and hoped one day to be in a financial position to marry her.

To his surprise, Laura burst into tears. Through her sobs she told Sydney her feelings for him were those of an older sister. Then she confessed that she was in love with a married man whom, she knew only too well, would never leave his wife.[2]

With horror it dawned on Sydney that Laura was talking about his father.[3] He felt sick at the thought of his father kissing Laura, was distressed for his mother, and regarded Frederick's behaviour as despicable. Sydney told Laura angrily that he could not bear to stay at Harker Lodge a day longer and left the room.

Sydney had always been close to his mother, but regarded his father as a "difficult" man, frustrated by his failure to become an opera singer, who enjoyed flirting with his female pupils. Now he felt nothing but jealousy and loathing towards him. Sydney provoked his father into an argument by declaring that he would not sit for the entrance exam for Oxford University, as had been planned. He would leave for Australia and stay with Arthur in Melbourne until he could find a job on the land. He would follow in the footsteps of his ancestor John Loch, who had made a fortune on the land and become a wealthy sheep farmer.

Laura, who was terrified that Sydney might reveal her secret to his mother, encouraged him to emigrate and gave him the money for a steerage class passage to Melbourne. His parents were upset at Sydney's decision but could not persuade him to change his mind. Sydney did not divulge to his mother the real reason he was leaving home.

Georgina darned Sydney's shirts and socks and bought him a second-hand dinner jacket, and a cousin gave him a set of tails. Before World War I, gentleman jackaroos were often invited to the Big House for dinner and were expected to dress for the occasion. Sydney also packed his favourite books and the typewriter Laura had given him.

Laura drove Sydney to Liverpool docks on 9 March 1909, and he boarded the SS *Suevic*, bound for Australia. He had only a few pounds in his pocket — he hoped the money would last until Arthur found him a job.

Arthur met Sydney in Melbourne and found him a job as a jackaroo on Kirndean Station, outside Albury, where he would work for a station manager named Blair.

As a result of the physical work and a healthy open-air life at Kirndean Station, Sydney had no more problems with bronchitis, which had once troubled him. He was soon a muscular young man and a crack shot; he also improved his riding skills and became an excellent horseman.

The elder daughter of the station manager, the pleasant but homely Elsie Blair, took a liking to Sydney, whom she insisted on calling "Sid". Together they went out riding; she enjoyed showing him around the property. Elsie acted as housekeeper for her widowed father while her young and immature sister, Jean, spent her time reading trashy novels. Jean did her best to flirt with Sydney, but he was not in the least interested in her. Kind-hearted Elsie invited Sydney to move from the station hands' rough and ready accommodation to the station manager's house and to join the Blair family at meals.

Elsie may have dreamed that one day Sydney would ask her to marry him. Although Sydney knew that his love for Laura was hopeless, he could not reciprocate Elsie's feelings for him. He saw that she was a sweet-natured young woman, who would make a marvellous wife for a man contemplating a life on the land, but he did not want to settle down with someone he did not love. He was restless, and hoped to travel around Australia. He also wanted to visit his brother Charlie, who was working at the Mt Cuthbert copper mine, midway between Cloncurry and Mt Isa, and to see the Great Barrier Reef, one of the wonders of the world.

Georgina wrote regularly to her son, but Sydney had no communication with his father. By now his mother was probably aware that her husband's interest in Laura was more than avuncular. She wrote to Sydney that Laura was not nearly as fragile as she looked, and was spending far too much money on cars and trips to the opera in London with his father. Sydney also learned that Laura's funds were running low, and she had started breeding Buff Orpington hens in the grounds of Harker Lodge as a commercial enterprise . . . and she was winning prizes and making some money from selling eggs.

Sydney's dreams were still haunted by images of Laura. He was torn between hating his father, pitying his mother and alternately loving and hating Laura. Yet he could not see himself marrying kind and devoted Elsie Blair; she was no replacement for Laura.

To escape from what he felt was now an intolerable situation, Sydney decided to leave Kirndean Station, return to Melbourne and stay for a while with Arthur le Paturel.

Shortly after his arrival in Melbourne Sydney was introduced to Arthur's cousins, the McGregors. They took an instant liking to him and invited him to stay at their home in Essendon. The McGregors became surrogate parents to Sydney.

It seems Laura may have felt guilty about the situation she had created within the Loch family and wanted to make amends through Sydney. Acting through her brother, she offered him a loan to purchase the lease of a large block of grazing land in Gippsland that Arthur had found, provided Arthur put up half the money out of his inheritance. Sydney was young and energetic, and could do the work of clearing and fencing the land and buying the stock, and all three of them would share the profits from any future sale, once a farm had been established there. However, Sydney would have to repay the loan in full if, for any reason, the lease had to be sold earlier.

In the long period of peace and prosperity before World War I, land prices were booming, and Sydney thought it wise to accept the le Paturels' offer. Wool prices were good, so it seemed he might be able to combine farming with a little writing, which was his passion. Sydney planned to work very hard for the next five years, establishing the farm as a going concern, then sell out and use the capital to support himself as a writer.

Acting on Arthur's advice Sydney bought the lease of a property in Gippsland known as Barwon Banks, near Morwell. It was 18,000 acres (7,465ha) of partly cleared land with two small houses: one would be for himself, the other one for a ploughman-cum-farmhand.

After two and a half years of backbreaking work Sydney was starting to make money from the proceeds of the farm. He needed a rest, though, so he planned a short holiday to visit his elder brother, Charlie, in North Queensland. Circumstances would force him to postpone his plans for several years.

On 4 August 1914, Britain declared war on Germany. En route to Paris, the Germans had killed hundreds of innocent Belgian civilians and raped women, and British propaganda spread the rumour that Belgian nuns were among them.[4] The British government, which had guaranteed Belgian neutrality, had declared war on Germany.

As Australia was part of the British Empire, Australia's Prime Minister, Joseph Cook, announced that an Australian Imperial Force (AIF) would be sent to train in England before joining the British Army to fight the Kaiser's troops in northern France. Australia was on the eve of an election, and early in September

1914, Prime Minister Cook's Liberal government was ousted; the new prime minister was British-born Andrew Fisher. The new Labor Prime Minister declared that Australia would defend the British Empire "to our last man and our last shilling".

Major-General William Bridges, Inspector-General of the Australian Army, insisted that the Australians would fight as a single force rather than being scattered among the British forces as they had been in the Boer War. Had General Bridges not insisted on this, there would have been no Australian Imperial Force (AIF) and no legend of gallant Anzacs at Gallipoli.

To join the new AIF, men had to be aged between nineteen and thirty-nine, but many boys lied about their age. Privates and gunners were paid six shillings a day, the wage of a working man — this was double the amount British soldiers were paid.

Recruitment was boosted by the fact that Australia was going through a drought, which meant jobs on the land had become scarce. Recruiting halls in every capital city in Australia were now swamped with excited volunteers, convinced the war would only last a few months and keen to join up. Enlisting was seen as the working man's chance to go overseas on an adventure at a time when there was no such thing as a tourism industry or cheap fares.

The AIF had announced that they wanted fit and able young men with some military experience, gained in earlier conflicts or the militia. It was assumed that this war would be like other colonial conflicts, swift, relatively simple and reliant on the bayonet and cavalry.

15

The lessons of the Boer War, which had demonstrated the importance of trenches and concentrated firepower, were largely overlooked. It was to be a costly error.

Young Australians feared that the war would be over soon, so they were desperate to enlist. Many of them had been raised on the land and knew a great deal about horses and had handled rifles since their boyhood. These raw recruits were physically tough and resourceful, and they imagined war as something like a football match, full of thrills and spills, where the best team won and everyone involved had a good time.

Most of the new recruits had British roots — in the 1911 census, 96 per cent of the population of 4.8 million regarded themselves as British, even if their families had lived in Australia for several generations. Apart from their appetite for adventure, many young men saw enlisting as their duty to defend the Empire.

Sydney Loch was young and idealistic, and he too was convinced that enlisting was the right thing to do. He had worked on the land in Australia for almost five years and felt that his future lay in this new country. He liked Australians and their sense of fair play, their dry, laconic humour and dislike of formality and ceremony.

Sydney asked the McGregors to write him a character reference, and enquired whether they had contacts in the Light Horse Brigade, or failing that, in the artillery. The McGregors approached Colonel George Johnston, a good friend. The colonel, a veteran of the Boer War, was in command of an artillery brigade at Broadmeadows Camp on the northern outskirts of Melbourne. Young Australians were being recruited and trained at the camp. Colonel Johnston promised the McGregors he would see Sydney and interview him personally.[5]

Lacking military experience, Sydney knew he had no chance of being made an officer like his brother Eric, who had graduated from Sandhurst Military Academy and would soon go to fight with the British in northern France. By now Sydney felt more Australian than British, so he preferred to enlist with the new Australian Imperial Force rather than the British Army.

EDITORS' NOTE

Sydney Loch's narrative *The Straits Impregnable* is recounted in the following chapters in a slightly shortened form, with the addition of selected photographs from the Loch family and other sources. As mentioned earlier, the book went through a number of editions with some differences between the Australian and British one. We have used the second Australian edition, abridging and editing it minimally, in line with suggestions by John Murray for a second British edition (see Epilogue). However, we took great care not to lose anything of Sydney's own unique voice.

For reasons mentioned in the Introduction, Sydney Loch changed the real names of almost all the persons featured in his book, including his own (the narrator's) name. Sydney's wit and sense of humour are demonstrated in his choice of pseudonyms.

Although most of the characters must remain obscure we have been able to identify the following:

- Lake (the narrator) = Sydney Loch
- Ted = Sydney's friend Arthur le Paturel
- General Runner = Brigadier-General Walker

- Colonel Jackson = Colonel Johnston
- Colonel Irons = Colonel Hobbs-Talbot
- Adjutant Yards = Adjutant Miles
- General Rivers = Major-General Bridges
- Captain Carrot = Captain Bean (war correspondent)
- Lieutenant Sands = Lieutenant Goodwin
- Corporal Tank = Corporal Furphey

THE STRAITS IMPREGNABLE

BY

SYDNEY DE LOGHE

[PEN NAME OF SYDNEY LOCH]

CHAPTER
ONE

PRELUDE TO WAR

Towards the end of August 1914, I went by train to Melbourne to meet up with my good friend Ted.

Ted drove me to Broadmeadows camp in a horse-drawn buggy. The wind had worked up into half a gale, and much of the way clouds of dust swept into our faces, so I crouched in the buggy, pulling my hat over my eyes. Fortunately, after we turned to the right at a crossing the buggy hood gave some shelter.

At last we saw the camp ahead of us. Tents stretched over many acres and there were paddocks filled with manoeuvring infantry and artillery teams. The road began to fill with infantrymen, some in uniform and others in civilian dress, marching in the opposite direction to the shouts of sergeants. A gun team and ammunition wagon rumbled past.

"This must be the place," Ted said and stopped the horses near the gate, which was guarded by a sentry. On the other side of the gate was a paddock filled with rows of tents, and between the rows ran horse lines. Guns and ammunition wagons were drawn up next to the road.

"I'll wait somewhere about here," Ted said.

At the gate the sentry challenged me, but I had obtained a pass to let me in. When I asked the sentry where I could find Colonel Jackson he pointed me in the right direction. Much was going on around me: men ran, trotted or walked; some joked, others argued or shouted. Tents were going up, horses were being picketed — things were topsy-turvy. Some men possessed military hats only, others wore military shirts or breeches, but the majority still wore their civilian clothes. Outside the quartermaster's store equipment of every sort was piled up, all looking painfully new.

After passing a line of tents I asked the way again and was directed to a large tent not far away. Outside that tent was a notice: HEADQUARTERS FIELD ARTILLERY BRIGADE. I asked an orderly, who stood in the doorway, where I could find Colonel Jackson. Without answering me he pushed up the flap of the tent to let me in. Inside the tent I saw three officers sitting at a table covered with papers and books; all three were busy writing.

The cap and shoulder badges of the man in the centre showed he was a colonel. The man to his right, a captain, was small, sharp-featured, and probably the colonel's adjutant. The two men went on writing, but the third, a lieutenant in his early twenties, looked at me and asked casually: "What do you want?"

"I came to see Colonel Jackson," I said.

The man in the centre put his pen down and answered, "I'm Colonel Jackson."

The colonel was a big middle-aged man, about fifty, and rather handsome. His hair was turning grey, his complexion was high and he looked as though he knew how to enjoy life. He looked me straight in the eyes. A good soldier, I thought, a man worth following.

"Yesterday I received notice from the Commandant at Victoria Barracks to report to you," I began. "I want to volunteer."

"What's your name?"

"Lake."

"Have you had any military training?"

"I'm sorry, none, but I can ride and shoot." And I added, "I hope this won't stand in my way. I'm very anxious to get in."

The colonel drummed his fingers on the table and looked at me for a while. In the end he spoke gravely, "You know, Lake, a soldier's life is hard — it's a very hard life: bad food, the ground for a bed, exposure to all weathers, work all hours. The officer is no better off than the man."

"I have not rushed into it, sir," I said. "I've thought it over and hope you will take me."

To this the colonel answered nothing.

I went on, "I've got some horses that would suit a gun team. I shall be glad to give them if they are of any use."

He misunderstood me. "Oh," he said, "we have enough now. In any case the Government does not give a high price. What do you want for them?"

"I don't want to sell them," I said. "I make an offer of them. They are plough horses, and if I go away there will be no ploughing this year. I am glad to offer them to the Army."

"Lake, I don't think there is any need for that. A man giving his own services is all that can be expected. Keep your horses . . . When can you come into camp?"

"I can come straight away, but I would like first to go back to Gippsland. I have a place there."

"That can be arranged." He turned to the lieutenant who first had spoken to me. "Sands, take Lake to the doctor and afterwards swear him in."

When out of the colonel's view, Sands pushed his hat onto the back of his head and stuffed both hands in his pockets. Then he led the way to the doctor's tent. But the doctor was not there, so we wandered about endlessly to find him. Now and then Sands would stop someone and ask when the doctor had last been seen — he always finished by swearing in a bored kind of way.

At last we were back where we had started: outside the big tent. "Stay here," Sands said before he disappeared inside. He came out with a large printed sheet of paper, a Bible, a pen and a bottle of ink. We took up opposite positions and made a start. The lieutenant asked endless questions, which I answered as well as I could. Then we came to the oath. "Take off your hat," he said while taking off his own. Next he handed me the Bible and we began the oath. In the blowing wind it was difficult to hear what Sands mumbled, so more than once he had to repeat the sentence. But we came through it safely — we wrote our signatures, which ended the ceremony. There was still the doctor's signature to get, but Sands was sick of me. He pushed the paper into my hand, waved me in the direction of the doctor's tent and departed.

I journeyed anew after the doctor and this time found him in his tent. He was alone, reading a long letter and smiling over it. He asked what I wanted, told me to strip and went on reading. He was still reading when I was ready, but presently he put the letter away and started to tap me. He tried my teeth, tried my eyes, and said I would do. While I dressed he filled in the papers.

I took the papers to the Brigade Office and handed them to Sands. Colonel Jackson was there as well, talking to another officer. "Captain Knight, I'm giving Lake to you," he said. "He'll be coming on Sunday or Monday, but first he is going down to Gippsland. Make him out a railway pass, will you?"

The captain, a well-dressed man with a restless manner, swung around and saluted. "Yes, sir," he replied. He told me to follow him along a row of tents and across horse lines. With me at his heels the captain eventually bounced into a tent where a sergeant-major and a couple of clerks were busy writing.

"This man has been given to us, Sergeant-Major. He wants to get down to Gippsland tomorrow. Make a pass out, please."

Then the captain turned to me. "When can you come, Lake?"

"Sunday or Monday, sir," I answered.

"Then come here Sunday morning. We've not much time and you ought to get all the drills you can."

I was given a railway pass, and left the tent with mixed feelings. There was no drawing back. I walked fast out of the gate, to where Ted was waiting for me.

"I'm in!" I called out. Ted grinned, drew the reins and together we returned to Melbourne.

The following day I went home to Morwell for the last time. The sun was shining and the day was very mild. Ted came with me and we drove in a hired buggy the eight miles from the station. Scottie, the ploughman, met us at the gate. When we stepped down from the buggy in front of the house the dogs jumped at their chains and greeted us frantically. I set them free for the last time. We unharnessed the horses and took them to the yard behind the shed.

"Have a look round the place," I said to Ted. "In the meantime I'll fix up things inside." Ted nodded in a dreamy way and walked off without a word.

Inside the house I opened all the doors and let the sunlight tumble in. I started to sort out all my papers and letters and threw most of them into the fireplace. Then I packed the few things I wanted to take with me, including some family photographs.[1]

After packing my things I went onto the verandah and sat down on the step looking towards the river. The sun shone over the paddocks, but the afternoon had grown cooler. There was little or no wind. The sheep were out of sight on the flats and the bullocks fed in the scrub far away. A few birds whistled to one another in the trees behind the house.

"Thus it was yesterday," I said to myself. "Thus will it be tomorrow, but I shall not look on — I watch this for the last time. My kingdom is passing into other hands. A stranger will sit by the fire at night. A stranger will read my books. A stranger will watch the

28

rabbit-fence and will count the cattle and muster the sheep. A stranger will hear the parrots whistling, the jackass laughing and the magpie yodelling. A stranger will mark the changing seasons and count the stars sailing through the skies. So be it."

After half an hour Ted wandered back. I chained the dogs up, kneeling to say a long goodbye to them. Maybe they understood, for they barked and scratched and jumped wildly. We put the horses to the buggy and climbed into it. Ted picked up the reins and flicked the whip, and for the last time we followed the track to the gate. Behind us the dogs were crying.

Old Scottie waited at the gate to give me a dirty hand.

"Goodbye, Guv'nor," he said. "Come back again."

"Goodbye and good luck, Scottie. Look after things, will you?"

That done, we went through the gate, rattling down the road. I looked back for the last time.

At the camp gate I said goodbye to Ted and he promised to look me up in a day or two. I picked up my bag, pulled out my pass and walked towards the guard at the entrance.

Rain had fallen the previous day. As soon as I was inside the gate I skated over a rink of mud, which appeared to be a feature of the camp. There were no signs of Sunday — all was hustle and bustle, and there seemed to be more men and more horses than on my previous visit.

There was no hurry as far as I was concerned, so I looked around from an island surrounded by mud. Eventually I went to the Brigade Office and waited there for my turn. It was not long before the clerk beckoned me inside, and for the second time I was before the colonel. He said a few words to me, but business soon took his attention. The orderly told me to wait for Captain Knight, who commanded the ammunition column. After a long time the captain finally arrived in a hurry. He was friendly and talked outside the tent with me for several minutes. He ended by saying, "From now on you are Gunner Lake. Come on. I'll hand you over to the sergeant-major."

He turned on his heels and away we went towards the column office. We passed the cookhouse on the way, where a long row of iron pots stood astride the fire. A rickety shed, furnished with a chopping block, basins and tools of the trade, was the cooks' only protection from the weather.

The sergeant-major, who was sitting in his office, took charge of me. I waited a long time while he went through some business with a clerk; by the time he pushed his writing things away and got up I was bored to death.

"Come on," he said, and we went outside. We slipped and slid in the mud and passed by men in all kinds of dresses. The horse lines were virtually impassable. The stout sergeant-major took matters calmly; I trailed along in his wake with my baggage knocking round my knees. We stopped at a tent somewhere near the middle of a row.

"Corporal Black!" the sergeant-major called out.

The corporal, a long, nervous-looking man, came out of the tent and stood to attention. The sergeant-major said, "This man is going into your tent. His belongings are with him and you can fix him up with the other things. Start him tomorrow. His name is . . . what's your name? — Lake."

After the corporal introduced himself to me the pair of them started to talk on other subjects — that is, the sergeant-major talked and the corporal agreed. When the sergeant-major left I was invited into the tent. Black showed me where to sleep and made me drop my kit there. There were bundles of blankets placed tidily near the entrance of the tent and several articles of clothing and equipment were hanging from the pole in the centre. None of the other occupants of the tent was present. Corporal Black sat down on a packing case and began to talk about the camp in general.

Presently he got tired of talking to me, so a lull fell between us. Then he remembered that I had not been issued with the regulation blankets and eating utensils. We went to the nearby quartermaster's store and I was soon loaded up with a waterproof sheet, a pair of blankets, cutlery and a pannikin.

The corporal told me I could do what I liked until twelve o'clock, when the horses went to water. So I started to explore within the artillery lines, looking at horses, guns, wagons, and everything else. Work had slackened off and men were washing themselves at the water taps, cleaning their leggings, or writing letters.

31

The whole camp, appropriately enough, overlooked a cemetery. I was not too exact over the tour because of the mud, so I returned to the quartermaster's tent and rested on a bag full of harness. Sitting there I saw a spectacle surely not equalled since Noah organised the march into the ark.

Along the road from the station, men, women and children came to the camp in thousands. They came in cabs, in carts, in motor vehicles, on horses, on bicycles or just on foot. All classes arrived to rub shoulders in the crush. Some were cheerful and some depressed. Old and young appeared: mothers, wives, fathers, children, uncles, aunts swept by in multi-coloured array. Baskets, boxes, parcels and handbags came with them, bulging with refreshments for the gallant volunteers. Outside the gate the road grew impassable from vehicles commandeered for the assault, and still more and more passengers arrived on foot. An army transport wagon tried to force a passage, but inevitably it jammed in the tide — neither the sergeant's threats nor his prayers availed.

The infantry lines swallowed up most of the invaders, but enough stayed behind to overflow into our grounds. I was sorry to see so many elderly people ploughing through the quagmire, but my pity changed to amusement when watching girls in silk stockings stepping through the mud.[2]

Twelve o'clock came and Corporal Black called out for me to give a hand with the horses. Men in the section were away on leave, which made us short-handed. The water troughs were at the other end of the compound, so in that direction we went. The rule was one man to two horses. There was a long wait at the troughs as an endless line of horses arrived at the same time. We stood in a couple of inches of water while the horses drank. Back at the lines, we tied up, heel-roped, fed and were dismissed.

Near our tent I ran into Captain Knight and Lieutenant Sands talking together. Knight called me over. "Lake," he said, "the colonel has made you his galloper, so you will leave the ammunition column and join the Brigade Staff. You're lucky, I would almost as soon have that job as my own. You have more chance of winning a VC than any man here." Sands grinned but said nothing. Knight finished up, "You'll stay in the column today and shift in the morning."

I thanked him and went on. It was good news and came as a surprise.

It was lunchtime when I arrived at the tent. An iron pot of greasy stew was outside, and Corporal Black ladled it out to the men standing with plates in their hands. I was introduced to the men, who belonged to the same tent as myself.

The stew failed to interest me, but it did not matter, for we were given no time to eat it. An order was announced: horses had arrived for us and we were to fall in at once. Everyone grumbled, but out we had to go. About a hundred men formed up in two ranks, and after the officers had deliberated at length we marched out of the gates at a smart pace. The crowd was still arriving from the station, though not in great numbers, but the road was completely blocked with waiting vehicles.

It was impossible to keep rank, and the order was given to fall out. The horses were in a yard by the road; after drafting them into pairs, each one of us led a pair back to camp.

The afternoon wore on, and by the time the horses were picketed, the trumpeter blew "Water" and "Feed". This brought the day's work to an end. After afternoon tea (bread, jam and tea) I went for a second journey of discovery. I watched a group of soldiers and some of the remaining visitors talking and embracing until closing hour arrived and the last visitors disappeared.

Finally the camp was empty of civilians. The stars came out, evening aged into night and the big enclosure was hushed. All that could still be heard was the impatient stamping of horses and the voices of pickets passing down the lines.[3] I found my way back to my tent.

I hollowed a hip-hole in the ground, spread out the waterproof sheet, and laid the blankets over it. I made a pillow of the clothes I took off and lay down. The other men drifted in and also made their beds.

I listened to the murmur of voices and watched shadows thrown from the one candle by the tent-pole. The trumpeter blew "First post", "Last post" and "Lights out".

At daybreak, reveille sounded through the camp. With the last notes I threw my blanket off and got up. The tent was open, showing a leaden sky where late stars hurried away. The horses stood with drooping heads in the lines and a picket wandered along at funeral pace.

In the tent no one had moved yet; all the breathing was even and serene. When I started to dress, Corporal Black rolled over and poked a nose out of his blankets. "Was that reveille?" he asked huskily. I nodded. He lay quite still, blinking his eyes, but presently he sat up and shouted, "Get up there, you fellows — reveille's gone ten minutes ago!" Right and left he leaned, shaking all he could reach. Slowly, and with many groans and an oath or two, the tent awoke. By now I was dressed, so I left the corporal to do his worst.

A second call sounded almost at once, and ten minutes later the "Fall in" went. From every tent men came tumbling, some without leggings, some drawing on their coats, half of the company with boots unlaced. Only a few arrived from the water taps with shining faces. We all headed towards the parade ground beside the quartermaster's tent. After falling in, the roll was called. Five minutes later the brigade marched to the stables.

The routine was like the previous day: watering, grooming and feeding. When we turned out, breakfast was ready: a small chop, bread and jam. After breakfast we paraded again for stables and exercising. Then along came lunch: stew, bread and jam.

I was sitting outside the tent, persuading myself we had finished a damned good dinner, when I saw a corporal standing close by. He was short, fat and very young. He came forward and began to speak in a hesitating fashion.

"You're Lake, aren't you?" he said.

"Yes," I answered while getting up.

"My name is Tank. I am corporal of the Brigade Staff. You've been put on to the Staff, you know, and I've come along to tell you to bring your baggage to our tent. We're in the four tents at the end of the row — if you come along now I can give you a hand."

I thanked him and collected my things. I told Corporal Black what was happening. The fellows in the tent nodded goodbye and then we left. The new corporal was quite good-natured and insisted on carrying some of my things.

A number of men sat by the Brigade Staff tents and looked at me with casual stares, but the corporal did not introduce me. He led the way into the second tent, which was empty except for blankets in their waterproof covers. "Take the place over there," he said, pointing at a vacant spot. I dropped my blankets and other gear where he suggested and while I did this he pulled a block of chocolate from his pocket, handed me a large piece and filled his own mouth. "You'll be all right," he said. "I have to go to Brigade Office now. We fall in soon, so don't go away."

After arranging my kit I went outside. The other fellows of the Staff still sat around in the tents, but as I knew none of them I walked towards the parade ground. It was getting bitterly cold again and half the men had their coats on. The horses in the lines were also rugged up.

I pushed my hands into my pockets, turned my back to the wind and started to contemplate my future, well aware that the situation I found myself in was of my own choice.

The trumpeter blew "Fall in" and I continued on to the parade ground. After roll call Corporal Tank marched us to the back of the Brigade Office tent and formed us up in two rows. Then he disappeared inside. Soon after he had left, the bitter winds tested our slender discipline. The men began to shuffle their feet and twist about, and next to break ranks. A pair started a boxing match, others played leap-frog. What remained turned spectators, or broke out into cursing the weather and themselves as fools for volunteering. Before long not a man was in his place.

Then, without warning, from the tent stepped forth dramatically Lieutenant Sands himself. He gave a preliminary stony stare before bursting into wrath. "What in God's name do you think you're doing? Is this a parade or a damned circus? I don't know how a lot of fools like you managed to join — you must have escaped from the nursery! Fall in at once! Next time all leave will be stopped."

The lieutenant had by no means finished. He tried indignation and failed, he tried sarcasm and failed, he tried appealing to our finer feelings and failed utterly. He became totally incoherent, and in the end gave up.

The corporal had followed Sands from the tent, but did not utter a word. He was carrying a bundle of white and blue flags, which he handed round.

"We're going to do station work this afternoon," Sands announced after blowing his nose. "Have you all got pencils and paper?"

Nobody had anything. "Oh, how absolutely damnable!" He beat the air with his clenched fist. "What do you mean by coming out like this? You are worse than babies! Go and get them. The next man that comes out without a pencil can consider himself under arrest." From the abashed ranks an individual wandered forth in search of pencils. Sands watched with darkening brow. "Double, man, double!" he screamed at last. The figure broke into a heavy canter and was lost among the tents.

While we waited, Sands and Tank held a conference. It was not possible to hear what was said, but at the end of it the lieutenant turned about with the order, "Fall out those men who have done no semaphore signalling."

Half a dozen of us, including myself, stepped forward. "Take these men, corporal, and start them on the alphabet. They won't need flags. See that you keep them at it — there's very little time for this sort of thing."

Tank saluted and cried, "Shun! Right turn — quick march," and away we went over the mud to a deserted corner of the camp.

"Halt! Left turn. Stand at ease," and there we were in line facing the corporal. "Pay attention," he said. In short jerky sentences he explained the principles of signalling, illustrating the position of "Prepare to signal", and other matters.

We prepared for the first circle: Ak to G. To prevent mistakes, A was pronounced Ak, B as Beer, D as Don. Away went Tank's arm, and away after it went ours, repeating the movements again and again. It was tiring and bitterly cold work, but we were kept at it. At last

Tank dismissed us for a few minutes' rest. The fellows wandered off in different directions, while Tank came over to me and started a conversation.

He struck me as a curious chap, dissatisfied with things, yet unready to make efforts to right them. I suspected him to be a poor disciplinarian, but he blamed the muddle on Sands, who, he said, was no good and heartbreaking to work under.

Presently the corporal ordered the signallers to fall in anew, which they did with considerable reluctance. Round and round went our arms again until the trumpeter blew "Stables".

That first week brought bitter winds and showers. Every day we had to stand in the open to practise signalling. At the end of three or four days there was no man who was not sneezing, sniffling and coughing.

Week by week it was the same thing. It was stables, stables, stables and signalling, signalling, signalling, with now and then a lesson on the director, plotter or range taker, and now and then a lecture. Lieutenant Sands gave the lectures in front of a blackboard in one of the tents. Halfway through he would often become tangled up beyond the vaguest chance of extrication. But that was small matter to him. He would go outside and read up what he had forgotten and come back and bounce us.

We also had riding drill and practised galloping in and out of action, and we were allowed to have some manoeuvres on our own account.

The camp endured several weeks of inclement weather and soon every man was sick to death of the whole affair. It was only our belief in the forthcoming departure that sustained us. Constantly it was rumoured that we were about to start on our great adventure; once or twice we even went as far as to make preparation. Disappointment was not borne in silence.

But at last it was going to happen. One dark and chilly morning in October we clattered through the Melbourne streets on our way to the wharf.

Our boat, the *Blankshire*, steamed out of Albany Harbour on 1 November.[4] The *Blankshire* was one of a fleet of transports at least fifty strong, convoyed by cruisers. We began a weary journey to an unknown destination. Fair winds and fair skies accompanied us. The fleet steamed in three lines, travelling at the fastest rate of the slowest vessel.

The *Blankshire* had steamed into Port Phillip Bay a fortnight before. We had left camp at the eleventh hour, so few friends were on the wharf to call goodbye. In the afternoon the band played on the boat's deck until the trumpeter blew "Stables".

At last land was exchanged for sea, but it was out of the frying pan into the fire. We moved into the swelter of the tropics and routine gripped us. It was stables before breakfast, stables after breakfast, stables in the afternoon and stable picket at night. Across the jumble of trampled men and nervous horses came forever Sands's voice. "You fellows, keep those horses moving. What are you doing there, Oxbridge? Why aren't you hand-rubbing, Woods?"

The procession of men and horses moved round and round the steaming decks — it was a battered, unsavoury collection. In the middle of the day, when the sun was most menacing, we rested for a couple of hours, lying about the decks to doze and read. After tea we loitered in the same way, and those who could brave the stifling lower decks went below to gamble. On pay nights you would find a gambling school at half the mess tables, with gold and notes passing forward and backward. Many a man left the table lighter in pocket but heavier in heart. Towards ten o'clock "Lights out" was blown, the hammocks would be slung on their hooks and we would turn in for the night, packed close together like sardines.

But who wants the details of that weary journey? Heat and the odour of manure are what I best remember of it. It seemed that never more would we sight land.

On 9 November the cruiser *Sydney* appeared on the horizon, and soon after we received the news that she had put the German cruiser *Emden* out of action. Unfortunately, we had been unable to see the fight ourselves. A great cheer went up — one of the few cheers that passed our lips for many a day.

Every evening a red hot sun went down into the ocean and a calm night would follow. Hundreds of hammocks rocked gently against one another on the stifling troop decks.

One day they inoculated me for the second time, and during the night that followed I lay in my hammock burning with fever. I turned and turned, but could not sleep. I saw the old sentry relieved by a new man who took his seat beside the lantern to read and nod. I remember waking and dozing, dozing and waking. Finally the night wore on towards morning and the fever began to wear out of me. It seemed at last I was wooing sleep.

Less than an hour would have passed when a great roar of waters, an unbelievable shock and a grinding of timbers woke me again. After an instant of silence the frantic hooting of the siren sounded. The sentry came falling down the companion with the lantern tumbling on top of him, leaving us in the dark.[5]

The shock of the collision had set every hammock swinging wildly. Being wide awake, I swung my legs over the side of the hammock and pulled the lifebelt down from the rack above me. All over the troop deck men had awoken and were reaching out for lifebelts while clinging to their hammocks to steady themselves. We were all frightened to death, and no one spoke.

Next a voice piped out: "Collision, boys, collision!" A score of other voices were making similar announcements. In the dark almost nothing could be discovered, but in no time men streamed up the companionway, fastening their lifebelts or carrying them under their arms.

I had wasted no time jumping onto the ground, but I did stop to put on my boots and overcoat, as I did not fancy the idea of a voyage in an open lifeboat in my pyjamas. Soon after the collision the ship became steady again, but the engines had stopped. As yet there was no sign of a list or any other problem.

Men who had slept on deck were trying to get down the companionway for their lifebelts while we, in much larger numbers, were pushing up. You heard men calling out, "Keep to the right!" or "Steady on there with your blasted pushing!" I was caught in the flood, which pushed me up the companionway and onto the open deck.

For one reason or another the deck was covered with water, and foolishly I thought, "By Jove, she's going down quickly!" I found many of the men with their lifebelts on lining up at their boat stations, where an officer in command called the roll. I hurried to my station, and there I found most of the Brigade Staff, with Lieutenant Sands in charge. He was quite cool.

Sands eyed me coldly as I fell into line. "Lake, you're too slow to catch your own shadow! Silence in the ranks! You fellows ought to know by this time that there is to be absolute silence. The next man who speaks will go under arrest."

It was a beautiful balmy night. The sky was full of stars and there was no wind. We had come to a standstill and the water about us was alive with sparkles of phosphorescence. All about us were the lights of the other transports, which seemed to have stopped. I peered into the dark to see whether anyone was coming to our rescue.

All men were lined up at their boat stations and the only movements were of the lifeboats' crews unlashing the tarpaulin covers and arranging the tackle and the oars. Suddenly a rocket went up into the air from our ship and Morse lights began to wink from neighbouring transports. Then a second rocket hissed into the air.

We stayed at our stations, whispering and shifting from one leg to another. But nothing happened beyond the turning of the stars, so a sense of security returned. Finally a hint of dawn crept into the sky. Sands, the unquenchable, marched solemnly up and down in front of us, his lifebelt drawn high under his armpits, which lent him the appearance of a hunchback.

Eventually HMS *Hernshaw* drew alongside, within hailing distance. She was a beautiful creature, but at the same time most forbidding. On deck stood an officer with a megaphone. "Are you all right?" There came an answer from our bridge, which I could not grasp. But the man-of-war's reply was plain to hear: "Then what are you waiting for?"

The *Hernshaw*'s searchlights had travelled up and down our starboard side. Apparently, our ship was not seriously damaged. Now the searchlights were shut off and the *Hernshaw* slipped away. Next our engines started to beat again and the screws began to turn. We were moving. There came the order, "Dismiss!" A half-light had crept everywhere and I could see men pouring down the companionways to the lower decks in pyjamas and shirts, talking and pulling off their lifebelts on the way down. On the lower deck, I ran into Sands, who had come down by another companion. Our eyes met and he gave me an understanding grin.

CHAPTER
TWO

IN THE SHADOW OF THE PYRAMIDS

After a month at sea we drew near the coast of Egypt. We held a concert on the ship's deck to celebrate our arrival. The stars were shining above us and the blue phosphorus-filled water was swirling below. To wind up our voyage Colonel Irons told us he had news to give: Egypt, not England, was our destination. There was work to be done and we might be fighting in a few days. The jaded company took heart again.

We lay off at Port Said among a fleet of war boats and other craft. Soon after, we were in Alexandria, and the long voyage had come to an end. A few days later we arrived at Mena camp, near Cairo.

When I awoke the morning after our arrival it was still dark. The sky was filled with stars although a pale streak on the skyline showed dawn was near. To our left reared the unmistakable outline of the Pyramids. The flatness of the country and the soaring sky above me seemed immense. Heavy dew had fallen, making the sand cold and damp. One of my legs had cramps and my back felt stiff from carrying my heavy pack. I got up slowly, stepped over sleeping bodies and stamped my feet to warm them up. There was no need to dress, as I was still in uniform.

Our horses were tethered to a single headline and lacked the heel-ropes we had used at Broadmeadows camp. Some lay on their sides without a twitch of the ear or a quiver of the nostril; others were stretched out breathing in great sighs.

Eaves, the wireless operator, was another early riser and together we helped one poor horse that was in danger of choking on a tangled headline.

By now light was spreading everywhere and the low-lying mist was lifting, but it was still cold. I waited a few minutes, hands in pockets, watching the new pickets move disconsolately up and down. Then I walked back to the sleeping members of our company. They were just as I had left them, lying under their greatcoats or blankets, many snoring heavily.

There was still an hour to go until the trumpet sounded reveille. Still feeling sleepy I lay down again under a blanket and dozed off. When I woke up for the second time that morning the sun had come up. Men were waking all around me, yawning, stamping their feet and cursing.

We formed a ragged island of men and horses, surrounded by a sea of fine sand. Nearby men and beasts had churned up the sand, but further away it sparkled virgin and unsoiled. The Pyramids rose up behind our camp, and beyond them the desert stretched away to the horizon. In the distance I could see a ridge of low hills.

Less than a mile away I saw a village of mud huts from which the sound of barking dogs could be heard. Tall white-robed figures moved among the palm trees that surrounded the village. One man led a string of camels and others sat astride tiny donkeys, their long legs sweeping the ground. Flocks of goats and sheep, tended by dark-skinned children, wandered through the village gate. Further to my right lay the road to Cairo, marked by two lines of poplar trees, along which we had marched the previous night.

Everyone seemed out of temper, blinking at one another and cursing as they struggled to their feet. Wilkinson, who hailed from England, a jolly vagabond and a liar of wonderful ability, asked, "What do *you* make of Egypt, Lake?"

I shrugged my shoulders. "So far, very little."

"Same here," he laughed.

Gunner Thompson chipped in, "What an awful place! Wish I was back in Collins Street." He rolled over and tried to go back to sleep.

Corporal Tank arrived and issued the command: "Get up! Fall in! Do you hear me, Thompson?"

"Yes, I damned well hear you," said Thompson, rising leisurely to his feet.

As the sun rose the world became more cheerful, but the bite in the air stayed. The horses had still not recovered from their journey and were lying still, with their bodies turned towards the sun. The pickets wandered back and forth along the line.

We had expected a day's rest, but instead we started what became the weariest day since we'd left Melbourne, as loads of chaff and many buckets of water had to be carted over the sand for the horses. The deep sand made walking laden down with heavy buckets a difficult task.

Later that morning we were told we had to move from our present position to the campsite allotted to us by the British Army, which had been there for some time. The new campsite was a considerable distance away and all our baggage had to be taken there. The many journeys through the sand, carrying all that heavy gear, seemed endless.

By mid-morning the sun was high in the sky and the sharpness in the air had gone, but the heat was not oppressive, as it was still winter. We were all dog-tired, and the endless marching across the sands was taking our spirit from us.

Some baggage proved to be too weighty for manhandling, so we trudged through the sand to the tented area occupied by the British, in search of assistance. The quartermaster's tents were rigged there and men weighed out meat, flour and vegetables, and loaded them on wagons. The crush in the lanes between the tents was unbelievable — carts, camels and soldiers were trying to pass through at the same time.

We found a line of rickety wagons, drawn by rail-thin horses whose drivers used frenzied gestures and wild shouts in an attempt to control their animals. Colourful language and promises of a good tip forced the drivers to thread their way through the throng. The drivers usually broke into a stream of passionate Arabic, followed by a cracking of whips and a grinding of wheels as they fought their way through the jostling crowd. Eaves and I stood there for a while watching the jumble of men and horses all around us.

On the outskirts of this animated scene, a score of camels quietly chewed their cud. The camel drivers could be seen squatted on their hams, eating small flat cakes they had cooked over a campfire. Their camels were thin and unkempt and the drivers were much in need of a good wash.

English soldiers from the Manchester Regiment had been sent from Cairo to help set up our camp. They knew well how to deal with the situation, and those who wanted a horse or camel-drawn wagon quickly chose the most promising of the worn-out beasts. It did not take us Australians long to learn how to secure our transport, ignoring the groans and protests from the drivers, who complained that they had worked all night and could do no more. We crowded onto their wagons and ordered the reluctant drivers to take us to last night's camping ground.

Matters improved a little with the help of the wagons. However, even with only a moderate load aboard the wheels sank deep into the sand, so we had to push and haul at the wheel-spokes or put a shoulder behind the wagon. The deep sand made the going heavy and we were sorry for the poor half-starved local horses, but we were even sorrier for ourselves. In that cumbersome and exhausting way the baggage was finally shifted.

A dozen Egyptians, under a European overseer, sank fresh holes for our horse lines. The transport of material continued through the afternoon and into the evening.

Our work as grooms continued until fresh chaff had been brought over and all our horses had been watered and fed.

Eventually Arab curses and Anglo-Saxon oaths got us installed in our new campsite. As yet the new camp had neither boundaries nor guards, so the Egyptians overran it. Numbers of them came to loaf and stare, including orange sellers, vendors of nougat, chocolate, picture postcards and cigarettes. Soon the trespassers would become a nuisance, but this was our first day and we accepted them in good humour and bought some of the goods they offered. News of the affluence of the new arrivals from Australia spread quickly. It was not long before the camp became a travelling bazaar, where merchants were waiting to bargain with the newly arrived foreigners, a chance far too good to be missed.

Egyptians passed constantly to and from the village on camels and donkeys, and cowherds and goatherds tended their flocks not far away. There was no false modesty: we stared at them and they stared at us. We saw brightly robed fruit sellers, money changers, guides, cigarette merchants, vendors of silks, chocolates, picture postcards . . . plenty of people with whom to argue and bargain.

There had been insufficient time to rig tents, so once more we lay down to sleep on the sand. The desert was not a bad bedroom, the sky being cloudless and full of stars. But as soon as the sun went down the night once again grew so cold that it made a mockery of our blankets and overcoats, with the result that most of us slept badly.

Mena camp grew apace. A huge triangular area, reaching almost as far as the Pyramids, became covered with tents as thousands more soldiers and horses arrived down the long road from Cairo. The infantry quartered themselves at the upper end of the triangle, where the floor of the desert narrowed to a valley and climbed into the hills. The Light Horse took the desert's inner edge, while the various service corps and we, the artillery, formed the base of the triangle, beside a grove of palm trees.

Steamrollers and gangs of native workmen flattened makeshift roads across the sands, reservoirs were built, wash troughs for the men and watering troughs for the horses were put up. Each day the camp continued to grow and improve.

Our first week was an evil one. We could not find our true position, so several times the horse lines were relaid. Our tents were pitched and re-pitched. And sleeping on sand was wearying beyond belief. We wondered whether a soldier's life would suit us.

About thirty of us slept in one large tent. Early in the morning light came in through the open doorways, revealing men tightly packed with arms thrown across one another and with their mouths open.

Reveille tumbled us out of bed on many a frosty morning. I say "tumbled us out of bed", but in reality most of us only turned on our pillows. Being slow at dressing, I usually sat up at the last notes of the

51

trumpet, as others were rubbing their eyes or lighting a cigarette. Many rolled over and covered themselves up again.

However, Corporal Tank's booming voice could not be denied, breaking the peace by calling out: "Get up at once! What are you doing there! Didn't you hear reveille called?"

A few minutes later his voice would rasp again. "Get up! Reveille's gone! I'll peg any man who doesn't get up!"

With many a groan and grunt and a few curses the whole tent would get up and stretch themselves.

It was wise to make an early start. Between "Reveille" and "Fall in" there was not much time to roll up blankets for inspection and stack our kits outside. As most fellows waited until the last few minutes to dress, there was great scramble and confusion. When the trumpet call for "Fall in" sounded, many of the men were still running about, dumping down their kits, putting on leggings and pulling on coats. After we fell in, standing in two rows, Tank called the roll.

Lieutenant Sands's habit was to stroll across and stand in the middle of the roll call, huddled up into his Army greatcoat, his face pinched and trembling with cold. The roll call over, Sands read brigade orders; at times, he added a few remarks of his own upon our sloppy habits.

Then came the first command of the day. "Turn in! Cast off for water!" The rule was one man to two horses, but more often it was one man to three or four. Those who stayed behind cleaned up the lines and filled the nosebags, and one man went down to the camels to bring up the day's fodder. The journey to the water was tedious and not without risk.

The vast congregation of horses was a wonderful sight. There were many thousands moving to and fro. On our way to the horses we would see the sun rising behind the trees along the Cairo highway. It was of immense size and blood red, and its long rays swept across the desert, setting the horses' backs shining. At once the chill left the sands, though the cold lingered.

Often there was a long wait near the troughs, as the water supply frequently gave out. Such times were spent calling to the other fellows, begging for cigarettes or watching the happenings at the village not far away. The place was full of Egyptian peasants moving about their work. Women went down to the waterhole, bearing on their heads large earthenware pots, children tended the flocks and herds, and men led camels and bullocks away into the palms to work at cultivation. There was always the shrill crying of voices and the barking of mongrel dogs.

In time our turn came and we moved on to the troughs. When the horses saw the water they made a plunge for it, and there was a breathless moment while they steadied down. They were given plenty of time to drink.

Then Sands's voice would sound again. "Staff, files left! Walk, march!" and we joined the great procession moving back to the lines.

On our return we heel-roped and began the morning's grooming. I rode a big bony horse named

The Director, who had known better days as a steeplechaser, and was now an honest hack. It was my daily penance to tend his wants and polish his coat, but my labours brought slender results. The desert sand was drawn to The Director like a magnet, and many a measure of special feed went down his throat without filling his hide. Yet I forgave him much, for he became a good friend.

The men on feed duty passed down the rear of the horse lines, placing a nosebag on each horse. Sands walked up and down the horses' heads, watching the grooms out of the corner of his eye. Here and there he stopped to make an examination. Often he suspected me and came up and rubbed his hand through The Director's coat. On unlucky days a shower of sand flew out.

"Lake," he would scream, "the condition of this horse is worthy of a court-martial. I thought you knew something about horses! It seems you never saw a horse before you came here! That's not the way to use a brush, man! Give it to me!"

Sands seized the brush and rubbed with great vigour until the dust entered his eyes and nose and left him coughing and sneezing. Then he fled to another victim and issued his next order. "In rear of your horses! Stand to your nosebags! Pick up your dressing on the right there!"

On such occasions Corporal Tank stationed himself at one end of the line and waved his hand in an agitated way. "Pick up your dressing there — pick up your dressing!" he would repeat after Sands in jerky tones.

Sands maddened most of his men, but he amused me. There was something likeable deep down in him. I am sure he saw the humour of what he was doing. Often I caught him smiling as he turned away.

When we were weary and the professional loafers had disappeared on one errand or another, Sands would start thinking of breakfast and call out: "Are you ready to feed, Corporal?"

"Yes, sir."

"Feed, trumpeter!"

And so the trumpeter blew "Feed".

Of all the good comrades who had come on this expedition and who could drive the devil of tedium from you, none was better than the trumpeter. He could tell funny stories with more wit than anyone else. He could act better, mimic better, dance better, lie better and laugh better than anyone else in our tent. In short, he could do anything that helped to hurry time. Night after night he was the centre of a circle of men shaking with laughter. If half his tales were true he had lived a strange life. The trumpeter was energetic, resourceful and had a stout heart; to a dispirited army he was worth a battery of guns.

There were other remarkable fellows on the General Staff — officers who had been educated at fee-paying schools, like Hawkins and pig-headed Jimmy Bull. There was Woods, who never looked dirty, and Stokes, who never looked clean. There was big Bill Eaves, who was always complaining but was an extremely kind man. There was Mossback from the bush, who had brains in place of education, and Corporal Baker, who was good at his work but would have been the better for a wash. There was Wilkinson, tall, lean and dark, and Lieutenant Lewis, tall and fair, with the face of a girl.

"Cookhouse" was blown soon after "Turn out".

In these early days we had no tables to sit at while eating our food. We squatted on our kitbags, plates on our knees, and chewed up sand along with our bully beef. The meals were rough and far from plentiful. Later we were given tables and forms and mess-houses were built for us.[6]

A canteen was opened near our lines, where you could buy a few extras for high prices, to supplement the eternal gritty bread. We spent a good deal of our money at the canteen, so at breakfast times we were emptying tins of sardines and salmon onto our plates. And it was, "Pass the bloody bread there!" and, "Fer Gawd's sake, pass the jam!"

For the first weeks after our arrival, orders forbade the riding of a single horse. At the cost of our legs we had to walk beside the horses when we were exercising them. We marched many miles a day, arduously tramping in the sand and coughing as the fine dust that hung in the air entered our nostrils.

The mornings were exhilarating and the days never grew too warm. As yet, there was no threat of the evil summer heat that was to follow.

Our journeys led us among the sand hills, where we were lost to sight of everything but dismal sweeps of sand. Or we would top a rise and see afar the palm groves on the desert edge and beyond them the great city of Cairo. To the right stood the Pyramids, and past them a vast stretch of desert, dotted with solitary palms or palms in groves; near the skyline were more pyramids. It was splendid to halt up there and overlook the country. The orange sellers, trailing gorgeous rags, followed us, and we might lie a few minutes sucking cool oranges, forgetful of the drudgery of everyday marches. Even Sands partook of the oranges and fell silent on these occasions.

Then we would return to the horse lines to water and feed our animals. In the afternoon we exercised the horses again. And this was the manner of our living during those first weeks in Egypt.

When you went past the guard at Mena House and turned to the left, you reached the long road to Cairo and fell into the arms of a passionate throng gathered outside the gates.[7] It needed a man of purpose to reach his goal undeterred. Brown frantic faces closed in — guides, donkey men, camel drivers, money changers, fruit and sweet sellers, beggars, fortune tellers, stamp dealers, postcard vendors, cigarette and curio sellers, silk and cloth merchants — one and all screamed and pulled at your arms for patronage. Restaurant price lists, advertisements of hot baths or addresses of friendly ladies were fluttered in your face. You were pulled to the nearest donkey, you were pushed to the nearest camel; a *gharri*[8] backed into your path and a motor hooted beside you.

There were raucous cries from the vendors.

"This way, Australia!"

"Australia very good, very nice!"

"Oranges, five for one piastre!"

"Nestle chocolate, only two piastres!"

"Donkey, sir! Or a camel, very good, very nice!"

And the reply was usually, "Go to blazes, the lot of you!"

The tram-car alone kept a dignified silence, for it was sure of patronage. It had but a single storey; and those who were cheated of room inside climbed atop and dangled their legs over those below. A shouting, singing, swearing company set off for the mysterious pleasures of the waiting city.

At last you found your way to a *gharri* or motor car, paid your fare, sank down inside, and with fierce cries from the driver, a crack of the whip or a sounding of the horn, you moved away from the throng. Dirty arms were waved in your face, but after a moment, interest in you and your money died and the gathering swooped upon new victims. You left the waiting row of camels and were soon eating up the miles to Cairo.

Along the way the road was filled with hurrying soldiers — trams full, *gharris* full, cars full of them. Soldiers hung their long legs over tiny donkeys, or rolled to and fro on camels. There were those also who walked, but in these early and wealthy days they were not numerous.

You'd pass army service wagons loaded up, platoons of infantry, peasants back from market, children driving home flocks of sheep and goats. Once I saw a solitary figure praying on a carpet by the wayside.

Further on, the countryside grew green and peasants were working among their crops. Now and again canals cut up the ground, and from them wandered away irrigation schemes so ancient, they seemed to have been there since Biblical times. There were waterwheels, put in motion by a listless bullock or two. Then quite suddenly you left behind the relics of past days and entered the fringes of Cairo.

Had you left camp towards evening, it would be dark by now. Tall houses with lighted windows frowned down and faces of all shades and dresses of many fashions were visible under the lamplight as you rattled past them.

Then appeared a quarter divided by broad thoroughfares with handsome shops and tall houses in the French style where the journey ended.

Cairo was full of Allied soldiers: Australians, New Zealanders and British. They seemed to own the place. Soldiers swaggered, hurried or mooched down every street, staring into every shop or exploring inside them. On every corner they were meeting and calling out, and every dozen paces they pulled up to examine the wares of native merchants. No article hawked through the streets or in the shops was too useless to find a purchaser. Some bargained for Persian carpets, while others bought charms or glass necklaces. Some fellows behaved like children in their delight, and the majority was orderly and well behaved.

Narrower streets and alleyways were dedicated to the business of everyday life. Until late in the evening men urged laden donkeys to go faster or bawled the virtues of their wares. Stale meat, rancid butter and vegetables lay on slabs in shops and vehement women bargained for tomorrow's dinner. You were buffeted and jostled and your senses were excited or sickened by sights and odours. The breath of the multitude was heavy in your face.

Those who were prepared to take the risk would leave the great lighted square, follow ill-lit arcades and turn one corner after the other into crooked lanes, filled with exotic smells, subdued cries and vague flitting forms. Tall, dirty houses leaned precariously over the alleys, leaving only a narrow strip of the starry sky visible.

From the wine shops the sound of cheap pianos could be heard and women could be seen through bead-curtained doorways. Many of these establishments were filled with soldiers and haggling merchants. In some dens you could catch a glimpse of a nut-brown woman belly-dancing.

Soldiers also invaded eating houses and cafes, and patronised with equal goodwill the best hotels and the lowest wine dens. When the stars overhead turned in their courses, many customers, stirred by lust and the wine they had imbibed, had different thoughts — the darker places of Cairo did not beckon in vain.

The cool of night found no way down into the narrow lanes of ill repute. In any of these places a hand might be laid on your shoulder.

There were many lanes to be followed and much wine could be spilled before you learned all there was to know. You could drift to the Bullring, where much was to be seen and done. But only the most daring or ill-informed went to the Wazir, where secrets would be unveiled in perfumed chambers.[9]

CHAPTER
THREE

"IF YOU WANT PEACE, PREPARE FOR WAR"

FROM *EPITOMA REI MILITARIS* BY VEGETIUS,
4TH CENTURY AD

Winter passed and spring followed, bringing fierce suns and scorching winds. By now we had learned to hate the country that once had amused us.

By day — and more rarely by night — we manoeuvred in the desert, making ready for the conflict that was so tardy in arriving. Life was hard, but I did not find it devoid of pleasure. I would gallop over the shining sands when the sun was scarcely awake, and spend my mornings perched on some observing station while batteries came in and out of action, heliographs flashed and flags waved.

Colonel Jackson proved a good master, though impatient and abrupt of speech. He spurred from point to point with half a dozen of the Brigade Staff on his heels, or sat in some trench on a hilltop, looking over the country with keen eyes. I soon learned the ways of the adjutant, a quiet man with little to say. On horseback the colonel moved swiftly about his business, covering many miles in a morning's journey.

Sands became a telephone expert and was to be found anywhere haranguing the cable cart men or kneeling on the ground, ear glued to the receiver of a field telephone. His conversations were worth listening to, including one he held at midnight in the desert. We received a report of a mock attack by infantry and Sands hurried to the telephone to call up Eaves, the telegraph operator at the next station.

"Eaves! Hullo there! Eaves, I say! Oh, damn and blast the thing, it won't work! Message for you! Eaves, are you there? Can't you hear me, man? Are you deaf? Message for you. Infantry advancing! Are you there, Eaves? Eaves, I say! Oh, blast! Oh, damn! Eaves, answer me at once! Lieutenant Sands speaking. Eaves, do you want to be placed under arrest?"

Meanwhile the unfortunate Eaves was walking up and down in the desert trying to keep warm, saying to anyone who would listen, "This game's no good to a man, keepin' a bloke 'anging round 'ere all night doin' nothin'. If the bloody relief don't arrive soon, I'm goin' 'ome."

Sands was a man in a thousand — there was none like him for cool effrontery, none like him for ignoring rebuffs, none like him for retracting statements without turning a hair. One fine evening he pulled me up in the stables:

"Lake, your horse is looking poorly. Is it getting extra feed?"

"Yes, sir."

"Well, *why* isn't it eating?"

"I was waiting for the command to feed, sir."

"Oh, man, you're a fool. I told you to feed that horse long ago. Feed it at once!"

"I thought the other horses would get restive, sir."

"Don't answer me back! Feed that horse at once!"

Next day he swooped on me as I carried The Director his extra ration of food.

"Lake," he screamed, "what are you *doing*? Are you *mad*?"

"I'm going to feed my horse, sir, as you told me yesterday."

"Man, you must be mad! You'll have the whole line torn apart if the others smell the feed! I thought you *knew* something about horses. Put down that nosebag this minute!"

With the coming of the hot winds the dwindling army of tourists departed for more kindly climates. As our own wealth had long since been squandered, the traders and night spots of Cairo were less interested in us.

However, Mena Camp had greatly improved. It now boasted picture shows, eating houses, hairdressers, even a bookshop and a tailor. But all these conveniences failed to assuage the seeds of discontent. The AIF was eager for war.

There came news of a Turkish dash for the Suez Canal and our Field Artillery was held in readiness. Hope of some fighting revived. But the attack came to nothing and we continued in our uneventful ways.

The sun grew hotter, the winds fell on us more fiercely, the flies multiplied. Men went about their work with bitter hearts.

Between the bugle calls for "Turn out" and "Cookhouse", Sands bore down on me as I loitered in the horse lines. Suspicious of his intention, I let him approach.

"Lake," he said, "Colonel Jackson is wanted at once at Divisional Artillery Headquarters. I want a man to find him now. The colonel went over to the palm grove with Major Felix. Saddle up immediately. Tell the corporal to keep your tea. I am sorry, but I can't help it."

Sands could even be polite when it suited him. With heavy heart I walked away to saddle up The Director. It was goodbye to my chances of tea. Any hope of success was small. A hundred roadways ran through the palms. The Director looked mournfully at his lost nosebag and followed me cheerlessly to the end of the horse lines, where I saddled him up and mounted. We travelled across to the place where the guns were parked. I was unable to get any information from the sentry as to the colonel's whereabouts, so I turned towards the palms, touched The Director with the spurs and he went away over the sands at a long, easy canter.

It was near the hour of sunset and the desert sparkled and grew rosy in the light of the dying sun. I dropped the reins on The Director's neck and let care slip away. My ill humour was departing. The desert was cool, empty and silent and the horse beneath me moved with the faintest hoofbeats on the sands. The camp was behind me and the palm grove was near at hand.

The sun fell over the forest of treetops, polishing them as a jeweller polishes emeralds; but there was not a breath of wind to move a leaf.

I passed into the palm trees near the village. The peasants had left their work and the herds were gathered home. A few children played among the trees and I called out, "*Saida!*" They ran up screaming with excitement. One or two I knew: Hanifa, Fatima and Habibi, the belle of the village. They could tell me nothing about the colonel's whereabouts. I scanned vainly for hoofmarks on the sand and chose a middle road leading into the heart of the palm grove, where from a low knoll I could see a considerable distance. The chance of success was small, but what better course was there?

Within the grove was cultivated ground. All these bright patches of green had grown up since our coming. Soon I lost sight of the desert altogether, except for a quick glimpse through the trees. The place was still, and filling fast with shadows.

I checked The Director to a walk, as speed was of no account — only luck could bring success. Never had I known the place so empty — no labourer bent over his cultivation, no driver led home his camels. Nor was there a sign of the men I sought.

However, the journey was not in vain. I caught sight of the colonel and the major, crossing the border of the desert land and moving towards the camp. They rode side by side and distance turned them to pygmies. I turned at a right angle to cut them off. No path led that way, but I made one of my own and now and then the

65

vegetable patches suffered. I spurred The Director on and cantered up behind them.

The major turned first, and next moment the colonel looked back. I saluted and the colonel returned the salute.

"You're wanted at once, sir, at Divisional Artillery Headquarters."

He answered something quickly; something not at all complimentary to Divisional Artillery.

We rode on without hurrying our pace — the colonel and major together and I a few lengths in the rear. At the edge of the camp we turned our horses for Artillery Headquarters at a fast walk. Then the colonel broke the silence and said, "I think we're away to the front at last, Lake."

"Thank God, sir!" said I.

"Thank God!" he replied.

We approached Divisional Artillery. The colonel said, "We should make a sprint to show our willingness."

And we spurred our horses over the last stretch of sand in a gallop.

The afternoon was well advanced when we formed up in the desert for the last time. We mounted our horses and passed through the camp towards the road that connected the Pyramids with Cairo.

News of our going had passed swiftly through the contingents of vendors we were leaving behind. They crowded either side of the way, giving us good speed with their cheers. The Director pricked up his ears and started skittering around, but a touch of the spurs soon brought him to heel. We clattered along the hardened way, nodding and waving freely to friends.

Everywhere voices called out.

"So long, old man."

"Give it 'em in good old Aussie style!"

"We'll be with you soon, Joe!"

"What's that, Jack!"

"Give the Kaiser a poke from me!"

"Look out there with that bloody 'orse. Mind my toes."

"So long, chaps! So long!"

I looked right and left, glad to be seeing Egypt for the last time . . . at least that was what I thought.

On our right stood a thriving town of tents, but on our near side the desert was bare as far as the palm groves. It resembled the scene when we arrived, eighteen weeks previously. A turn in the road and we had left behind the tented area and were winding between the picture shows, the native bazaars and eating houses. The crowd thinned. At Mena House Hospital the guard fell in to present arms. Next, before one could count ten, we were turning to the left and streaming on to the road to Cairo. The desert was left behind as a memory.

There was the usual ravening throng of guides, camels, donkeys, money changers, fruit sellers, carriage drivers and touts and the continual side play of nervous horses. Then we were out beyond the tumult and into the quiet, sweeping along an endless road, fringed by two straight lines of poplars.[10]

The sun had descended and now tossed immense shadows over the country. I rose in my stirrups to gaze a long while at the Pyramids. The wonderful masses of stone stood as they had stood at our coming; and they still possessed the same power to awe me.

Abruptly I turned my gaze away from the Pyramids and looked down the road. Colonel Jackson was looking backwards towards the camp. "I never want to see that place again!" he burst out.

We had started in good time to catch the train, so there was no hurry. The end of the column was not yet in sight. We kept to the right, to avoid a passing tram sending some of the horses across the way. Once a dozen Army service wagons rattled by with forage aboard. Sometimes evil-eyed camels had to pass, as well as herds of native cattle and flocks of shorn sheep, herded by children. Sometimes a motor car tore out of the distance. But these meetings were few and far between on the long road.

"March easy" was blown and caused a great pulling out of pipes and cigarettes. Hawkins rode beside me. The trumpeter trotted back down the line, in time for a cigarette. He stuck it in the corner of his mouth, winked and did his usual mock Shakespearean speech.

"Hail, most noble one. Sallyest thou forth to the field of battle?"

The trumpeter broke off to snatch the match from Hawkins's hands and light his cigarette. Drawing a deep glow, he struck his chest with a noble gesture.

"I shall return to my post in the van. Farewell and God speed, valiant sirs!"

Egyptian peasants stopped their reaping and their watering to watch our passage and started chattering among themselves and laughing. They seemed as light-hearted as we.

The column continued at a walk, so men would shoot a glance towards the officers and, being unobserved, would break rank and trot up or drop back to some particular friend. Up and down the column one could hear the same appeal.

"Give us a cigarette, mate. Not 'ad a smoke all day."

"Mate, can I have a match?"

The clatter of thousands of hoofs and the murmur of many hundreds of men set me wondering what would happen. A month hence, how many empty saddles would there be? How many riders mourning their steeds?

"Gunner Lake, Gunner Lake, enough of such depressing thoughts — the good soldier does not think," I told myself sternly.

Shadows deepened, evening drew in and the sun set. The miles were eaten up and all of a sudden the country ended and we were clattering through the suburbs of Cairo.

The clamour of our going echoed into the gardens of private houses and into the upper apartments. Pale faces, olive faces, brown faces peered from windows and over balcony rails — heads with hair piled high in the latest French fashion, heads supporting pigtails bound with bows and heads crowned with red fezes. Heads of raven hair I saw, heads of brown hair, heads of silvery blonde. Many girls sent us a smile, but the old men looked on without much interest, having seen armies before. Forward we went, and the traffic in our path had to bunch itself on the side of the road. It grew darker and darker, until only dim forms could be seen. Lights were shining through countless windows from the houses along our way.

An order came down from the head of the column.

"Halt!"

At once there was tightening of reins and the drivers lifted their whips in the air. You could see the signal passing down the line: "Prepare to dismount . . . Dismount!"

I did so and pushed my fingers under the saddle girth to feel The Director's belly. He was hot and steamy, but otherwise seemed well. I gave him a friendly smack on the rump and left him.

Some men sat down on the curb stones and started to munch chocolate or biscuits or whatever food they had with them. Our rest break did not last long.

"Prepare to mount . . . Mount!" came the order.

In five minutes we were off again.

We came to a bridge bearing great lamps. Beneath it flowed the ancient, ageless Nile. Countless native boats lay along the shores. This was the river that had rocked Moses, and the barge of Cleopatra had floated here. But now an armoured company of men streamed across it, hoping to write a few words in the pages of history.

It was dark when we came into the town itself and neared the railway station. This way and that way we flowed through the twisted streets, bringing the girls to

70

the windows and the shopkeepers to their doors. The better quarters we did not see, for we followed back streets haunted by strange smells. Half the shops were eating houses, where Egyptians smoked and drank coffee while playing dominoes or backgammon. Some looked up and peered out at us, but I do not think that the blessings of Allah followed us every time.

We reached a business quarter, hedged by brick walls and with narrow lanes abutting. Here we joined other bodies of troops bound for the same destination. Above the jangle and clatter sounded the whistles of engines and the bumping of trains. We passed under a gateway and came to the station.

The head of the column clattered into the courtyard and removed their saddles. In no time the place was crowded with soldiers, horses and vehicles. The square was in deep gloom and chaos took charge. There were two entrances to the square: a dim one leading from the streets, and another one, lit by an overhead lamp, with a ramp that led the horses up onto the station platform. I received a hazy idea of all this before being caught up in a whirlpool of activity.

Men hurried this way and that, men shouted to one another and cried out orders or swear words. Nervous horses stamped, bumped and side-stepped. Now and again there was shouting: "Gangway here, gangway there!" or "Get out of the way!" There was rattling and jangling as the guns were pushed towards the platform and the waiting trucks.

Members of the General Staff found themselves pushed to the edges of the courtyard, some of them holding three or four horses. Others were unstrapping nosebags and pushing them over tossing heads. Saddles were packed away in grain bags, specially brought for that purpose.

The night became dense with steam from the horses and the rank odour of manure. The stench, the jumble of animals and the weight of packs and marching gear on our backs did not help matters. Every few seconds some horse would swing its quarters around and barge against you, almost knocking you down. It was "*sauve qui peut*" — "every man for himself".

Sands was all over the place, ordering, expostulating and reviling. His movements were greatly restricted by his sword, revolver, haversack and the other impedimenta he carried.

"What are you doing there, Thompson? You're as useless as you are fat!"

"Lake, you're the slowest man in Egypt! Hurry, man, hurry!"

"I told you not to pack those saddles that way, Eaves! You're the stupidest man I know!"

And then he would disappear in a riot of curses and someone would mutter, "I hope he's done himself in for good and all!"

The slender patience of the General Staff failed under this trial, as did that of the men. Out of the darkness rose an Australian voice.

"A bloke ought to get six months for coming on a fool's game like this! Do they think we're slaves? Blast the bloody Empire!"

"Fer Gawd's sake, shut yer row!"

"No, I bloody well won't!"

The watering, feeding and manoeuvring of horses took a long while because it was almost dark, but finally all the nosebags were properly fastened. The clattering of hooves abated, though more hard work lay ahead. Saddles had to be forced into bags that were too small for them. I was able to escape to the platform on some urgent business. Hurry and confusion triumphed there as well, but it helped that the area was lit. And there were no horses, which helped even more.

The train was drawn up to the platform — coaches for the troops in front, horse-boxes next, trucks for guns and wagons in the rear. The platform was in military hands, except for one secluded corner where girls said goodbye to a sergeant and a corporal.

Already the trucks were loading — on one I found our telephone wagon. Further down, soldiers were hauling the cook's wagon aboard.

The place was as busy as an anthill and as noisy as a rookery. Gangs of men swept to and fro, carrying baggage on their shoulders, and hauling vehicles aboard the trucks with cheery cries and yo-ho-hos.

Officers stood at fixed points to wave hands and direct, while sergeants and anxious corporals saw to it that there would be no rest for us soldiers. Many grumblers threatened below their breath, and many took advantage of the general confusion to disappear to the bar in search of refreshments.

There were shrieks of engines and much jolting and jarring and snorting of steam engines. One engine was in the process of coupling with our train. Before long a chain of our fellows came into view with the bagged saddles on their shoulders; a line of horses on their way to the ramps, which led to the trucks, followed behind. I saw them too late and was seized to lend a hand. The office was no sinecure, and I had to play the acrobat more than once to keep clear of so many horses' heels.

We had arrived at the station in good time, but when I looked at the clock the hour had grown late. Much remained to be done. Nearly all the horses and all the heavy wagons were aboard, but quantities of lesser luggage kept arriving on the backs of blaspheming men. I had little time to look around as a thousand errands were given to me. I went outside again, and found that the courtyard was still blocked with waiting men and horses. On the platform I ran into members of the General Staff who were trucking the last horses — once again I was ordered to give them a hand.

Trucking and baggage loading finished together and we were ordered to fall in for another roll call. Three times the roll had to be run over before all were present.

It looked as though we would have breathing space at last. I was starving, and borrowed a couple of shillings to buy some food, but the chance of feasting had passed. Signs were everywhere that the hour of departure was approaching, and further freedom was denied. As yet the platform had not emptied of people; men stood about in groups, wiping perspiration from their foreheads.

"Right turn! Left wheel! Quick march!" and away we went towards our carriages in the train.

"Aboard there — all aboard," came the order.

We pushed through the narrow doorway like schoolboys.

The carriage was in second class, and not over-clean. There was a scramble for seats. I found one near the centre of the carriage under a dingy light — fortunately, it was close to a window, so I could look out. The men began to rid themselves of their marching gear, which weighed on them like millstones. Although there were seats for all, there was little room for feet or equipment, which started many arguments. By the time the gear was stacked we were no better off than sardines in a tin.

Although the business of settling took time, events moved rapidly on the platform, and without warning Sands appeared on a final tour of inspection. He told us that the train would start in a few minutes and threatened anyone leaving the compartment with immediate arrest before going away to his own first-class carriage.

A man with a tray of very ancient pastries put his head in the door and loud bargaining and a good deal of pushing ensued. The clamour continued until the guard blew his whistle.

After the first whistle came a second and then the noise of releasing brakes, followed by a jerk, a jolt and another jerk.

A cheer went up and a hundred arms waved from the windows as we moved away into the darkness and the station platform fell away behind us.

Immediately after all this tumult some strange moments of quiet followed, as though the fact had dawned that we were starting a journey that would be the last for many good fellows. But the moment was only fleeting. Men continued finding their seats. Some searched through their gear in an attempt to find something for supper.

After five minutes we bumped noisily through the town.

I peered through the window and saw lights come and go and flashes of unfamiliar scenery. I saw houses set in gardens of palms and at a level crossing I saw a native and his camel waiting in lazy patience.

Beyond the town we passed through shabby suburbs before we entered flat, open country. There were no more lights, so very little could be seen. Here and there shadows pointed to the sky and vague outlines of huts and hamlets sped into a square of light and out again.

I soon tired of peering into the darkness and found some supper — iron rations of tins of bully beef and biscuits. I had one tin of sardines left and fared quite well. We loitered over supper and afterwards some men started to gamble and others went off to sleep. Apart from the arguments of the card players there was little conversation. Jerking and clanging, the train rumbled on through the night.

I began to yawn and lay back, then became drowsy and nodded off.

Later I woke up and saw the rowdy gamblers and other men who dozed, like myself. At last I must have fallen fast asleep.

When the stars paled before a cheerless dawn my circulation and spirits were at their lowest ebb. The train drew up and emptied us onto the platform at Alexandria, the port where we had arrived four months ago.

We re-enacted the previous night's activities. We stumbled onto the platform with bag and baggage and fell in without ado. Then the roll was called. On the horizon the sky was cold and grey and the last stars faded. Yet while we stood there we saw a faint colour creeping up in the east, and it gradually revealed a forest of masts and a score of sails of native boats.

But this was no time for contemplation.

"Shun! Right turn! Quick march!" was our portion. And away the gallant band marched to unload horses, to gather up saddles and other gear and perform endless fatigues. Daylight was abroad long before we finished. What remained to be done was watering and feeding the horses, but there was no mention of our own breakfast.

The harbourside was filled with transports, ready to go out to sea. All signs were here of a mighty expedition. From train to wharf — where our ship, the *Hindoo*,[11] lay moored — was a relatively short distance.

Cranes screamed and rattled and men swarmed onto the decks or ran up and down gangways. The *Hindoo*, a good-looking vessel, was three parts loaded and ready to sail that night. The wharf where she lay was blocked with horses, guns, limbers and all the other baggage of war. To the left of us a French colonial mule corps had gathered, and past it was the French airship transport corps.

We were fully loaded by evening, and then the rattling of dripping anchors fell about our ears. I stood on deck above the emptying wharf as the colonel passed by. He stopped, smiled and said, "Off at last, Lake" and I saluted and said I was glad.

Slowly the ship drew away from land — fathom by fathom widened the band of water from the quayside.

In the middle of Alexandria harbour we turned about and steamed out into the open sea. The lights on the shore disappeared and Africa was no more.

The propeller thumped and churned while we moved into the ocean towards an unknown destination.

CHAPTER
FOUR

TO THE DARDANELLES

It seemed that at last our ship was drawing into a port. Nearer and nearer it approached, until the waterway narrowed to a ribbon and an unknown island presented cliffs and beaches, shelving smoothly down to a turquoise sea.

Many aboard declared we had reached the Dardanelles; others thought we were at Tenedos. Some were certain we were approaching the island of Lemnos.

All we could do was watch and wait as we found ourselves moving parallel with the shore. Sunbeams flecked the land and swept across small cultivated fields. We steered beyond the cape and two great jaws of land opened wide. Inwards we steamed. We had entered a large sheltered bay where green hills climbed from the sea, patches of cultivation marked the easier slopes and hamlets clustered in the shelter of the valleys.

A mighty fleet lay at anchor in the landlocked water — two fleets, in fact: a battle fleet and a fleet of transports. It was a wondrous spectacle to come across in the Aegean.

And so on 4 March 1915 we arrived in Mudros Harbour.[12] Across the mouth of the bay a net had been drawn so that no enemy submarine could enter.

Grim battleships lay there, and swift cruisers, their grey sides shimmering in the sunlight. Black destroyers lay anchored beside them. A half-submerged submarine, with the crew on the conning tower, passed down the thoroughfare. Trawlers, tugboats, lighters and mine-sweepers all lay anchored before us. Giant liners swayed their cables and showed decks crammed with men in khaki uniform.

The noblest of all was the HMS *Queen Elizabeth*, with her powerful fifteen-inch guns. She moved through the lines into the outer bay, then gathered speed and churned towards the Dardanelles. Only a broad wake remained to mark her passage.

Slowly the days went by and still we lay at anchor in the sheltered waters of Mudros Harbour. Impatience was growing with each rumour and delay. New transports continued to arrive.

Each day the bay became more crowded and there were reports of even more transports on the way. Fresh rumours were born each morning. We were to weigh anchor tomorrow. We would remain here for a fortnight. Now Turkey had discussed terms of peace and we were no longer wanted.

Each day saw a similar program performed: stable duties, mucking out, watering and feeding our horses. Grumbling flourished.

I never quite shook off the glamour of that island in the deep blue of the Aegean. Never was there an early morning when skies were not blue and waters unruffled. Breezes softer and more scented than human kisses floated perpetually to us from the hills of Lemnos. Every sunrise brought the same scene, with gigs, cutters and small boats plying between the giant ships. Against our sides bumboats would collect, handled by wily Greeks with offerings of tobacco, dried fruits and nuts, Turkish delight and chocolate. Business was always brisk until whiskey arrived aboard; afterwards the bumboats came no more. The magic of those mornings has stayed with me.

There were days when the battleships left the anchorage. The smaller craft, such as the destroyers, were active at all hours. Hither and thither through the lines they moved at speed, coming and going on their journeys.

Many an evening the sun went down behind shadowy hills which circled a bay of glass, whereon destroyers had ceased to manoeuvre and the last rowing boats were pulling for home. As the shadows lengthened, often a submarine churned past us, conning tower awash, like some strange monster of the deep.

Once the day's work was over men gathered on deck for the breezes, which revived about this hour, or settled below to gamble until the "Lights out" trumpet was blown. The hills would retreat into the distance, the water would turn to grey and the great boats would give up their shape. The stars looked down to rival them, a thousand lanterns shone forth upon the waters. Far into the night winked the Morse lights. "Dot, dash, dot, dot, dot, dash."

Sometimes we held sing-songs on the deck below the bridge. B Battery had a song by a poet of sorts, which always scored encores and ran like this:

We are the boys of this good Battery,
The joy and the pride of the Artillery;
We do not like work; but what soldiers do?
And we're after the Turk on the good ship *Hindoo*.

Later on men appeared with their bedding — a blanket and a rug, with a coat or something of that sort for a pillow — and put it down in an unoccupied space. The groups about the piano would thin. Before ten-o'clock lights on the troop deck went out, the men turned in to bed and conversation died to whispers. So another day of waiting ended. Often I would lie awake to stare up at the chilly stars, or watch the tireless winking of the Morse lights. At those times thoughts of death knocked at the doors of my brain.

At last it seemed our waiting was over. Rumour became persistent and less vague. Something of the plan of campaign was announced. We were detailed about our duties and our places in the barges were allocated. Having been appointed as the colonel's orderly, I was given a place in the first barge that would leave the ship.[13] I took heart from that decision.

The plan of attack was this: the Frenchmen were to land at Kum Kale [Canakkale] on the Asiatic side; the

82

British at Sed-el-Bar, opposite. The New Zealanders and ourselves would pass beyond the British and attempt a point somewhere near Gaba Tebeh [Gaba Tepe].

A fleet of mine-sweepers was in the vanguard of the expedition, with cruisers to follow to cover the destroyers bearing the infantry. Behind came the artillery, and behind them yet other units.

The approach would be made by night and the attack launched at daybreak. The artillery transports carried two batteries from one brigade and a single battery from another, with the idea that two boats might unload together and a complete brigade be put ashore in record time. All horses would remain on board for a day or two at least.[14]

Such were the meagre details we received, but we were told everything had been considered, and the coming battle would prove among the greatest in history.

On the afternoon of our last day at Lemnos there came a rattling of anchor cables and the murmuring of turning screws, and suddenly our ship was moving down that crowded thoroughfare towards the open sea.

We were amongst the earliest transports to move; the fleet followed us in single procession. On both sides of us decks filled up with khaki-clad men and there was the sound of voices. Solemnly we moved along the row of ships. We passed many noble craft of war with cold grey sides and polished guns and several splendid liners carrying almost an entire township of men. Through the newly opened submarine net we steamed into the outer bay. Our engines slowed again, cables roared and rattled anew and the anchors plunged into the sea. Here we were to wait until the final hour.

More ships anchored in our neighbourhood while others steamed on towards the horizon — there seemed no rule, no plan. The sun sank down and ocean and skyline met in a clear rim. The cruisers, which had to guard us through the night, looked like tiny specks silhouetted against the light.

The sun's rim dipped below the horizon. Close to starboard lay a French trooper, anchored, and nearby clustered a fleet of pinnaces towing long lines of open boats. We were wondering at the meaning of the sight when word arrived that the French would practise a landing. The boats filled with men, the signal was given and the pinnaces steamed at speed for the shore. Like hurrying serpents they swept through the oily waters to meet the land as dusk descended.

Against the glowing sky I noted the heads of the men moving above their huddled bodies and the thin rifle barrels bristling everywhere. One could not see their faces, only imagine them.

Down went the sun. Upon the ocean, lamps came out, and more lamps came out in the sky. The hospital ships with their green and red lights glittered like fairy palaces. All evening and well into the night boats threaded their way out of the harbour. The hours went by. "Lights out" was blown. Upon the quiet ocean a navy and an army rested. Yet many men stayed restless, dreaming of the dawn.

I was on stable picket. About seven o'clock I carried my blanket down onto the horse deck and laid it out on the hatchway between the bales of lucerne. The overhead hatch was open, so I could look straight up into the sky. The stars shone lustily and soon part of the moon would be visible. Even though the hatch was open, the air below was close and musty, for there was little wind abroad and none found its way down here. Most of the horse deck was in darkness. A single electric lamp hung low over the hatchway for every man to knock himself against with an oath.

The horses moved wearily in the stalls, rattling head chains and stamping impatiently, as tired of the voyage as ourselves. Now one rubbed itself endlessly against the bars of the stall, now a mare snapped spitefully at a neighbour. Everywhere dwelt the musty odour of manure and stale hay.

The other pickets sat by their lines, talking and smoking and keeping a watchful eye on the companionway in case the orderly officer turned up. I walked up and down, patting some of the horses and calling out to those known as biters and kickers, feeling as restless as the worst of them.

Presently I sat down on a bale of lucerne and dropped my chin on my hands. All my thoughts were of the morning. The rattling of chains and the shuffling of feet went on. My thoughts travelled further and further from the present, until the horses and their ill-temper were forgotten.

Then steps came down the companion ladder. The pickets sprang to their feet, hid their cigarettes and started to pace up and down. The alarm was false. Lieutenant Campbell had arrived to look at his mare. He came round to where I sat, patted his horse's shoulder and started to call her pet names. Then he saw me.

"Evening, Lake," he said. "I came to have a look at Bonnie."

"Have you any news, sir?" I asked.

"Yes. We leave at midnight. At four o'clock we pass the French landing and at five we shall see the British. The infantry have started already."

"Thank God we're making a move at last," I said.

"Yes, Lake," was his answer. He laughed and added, "Good night, Lake." When he went up the companion ladder I sat down again on the bale of lucerne.

I was surprised to find how fast the time had gone, for my relief arrived a few minutes later. We talked for more than half an hour and then I went to bed, rolled up in my blanket and started to read a magazine. I read and read, feeling unlike sleep. The heavy air and monotonous noises made me drowsy, but still I could not sleep.

The picket that had relieved me was relieved in his turn. I finished reading the magazine, threw it aside and lay back, yet I felt less like sleep than ever. Overhead the stars had circled halfway round the sky. They were less bright, a sign that the moon had come up. Surely it must be midnight.

Just then came movement overhead, a turning of winches and a grating of cables. We had weighed anchor for the last time.

Up jumped the pickets, shouting: "We're off, boys, we're off."

One ran up the ladder like a monkey and climbed onto the upper deck. Presently he poked his head down the hatchway and into the light. "We're off all right — it's dinkum this time!" The screws started to turn and the boat began to throb. The movement woke the horses and set them shuffling in the stalls, and with new energy they rattled their head chains. I lay on my back and stared ahead, trying to predict the future. Would the Book of Death be opened wide and my name be written there?

I awoke quite late on the morning of 25 April and looked through the open hatchway at the sky, which was just starting to light up. A pleasant breeze found its way down and drove off the musty odours of manure and pressed lucerne. For about half a minute I lay thinking of nothing much, hearing in a far-off way the shuffling of the horses. Then all of a sudden the business ahead of us came into my brain like a thunderclap.

The deck above was full of men who had come up for their morning wash, carrying towels around their necks and soap in their hands. But instead of washing themselves, all looked in one direction — the landing, of course.

Up went my head, listening for the guns, but I was unable to hear them. Within three minutes my toilet was finished and I went up the ladder two rungs at a time. On the deck above I found myself surrounded by a big crowd. I made my way to the rail.

A stiff breeze was blowing and there was salt in the air. Considering the breeze, the sea moved very little, giving promise of a fine and clear day. However, it was not light enough to see the horizon properly. Even after a sharp look around I could distinguish nothing.

I came across Gunner Wilkinson and Gunner Lancashire, chatting together. "Can you see anything?" I asked.

"No, there's nothing doing yet," they answered.

"I thought we were to pass the French about four o'clock."

"We passed them a long time ago, but too far out. They're looking for the British landing place now, but I heard a bloke say we wouldn't pass it before breakfast."

I went onto the troop deck for a towel and soap. There were still a good many fellows rolled up in their hammocks or sitting at the mess tables. Anyone awake wanted to know what was going on, but hearing nothing, they settled down again. After my wash I went to the parade deck, leaned over the rails and listened in vain for the guns. Then the trumpeter blew the call for stable duties.

We spent an hour in the stables doing the usual things. On the way to breakfast there were still no signs or sounds of battle. The horizon was quite clear of battleships — or any craft at all. The sea rolled away on every side.

We had curry for breakfast. There was less of a scramble than usual, as a number of fellows stayed above, hoping to see or hear something. Others were too excited to have any appetite. For my part I ate well, not being certain when I would get my next meal.

After breakfast I went up on deck again. At least half the boat's company was hanging over the rails along the starboard side. I edged my way among them, asking what was happening.

"Can't you hear the guns?" someone said.

There was absolutely nothing to be seen, so I put my head on one side and listened. But I could distinguish nothing beyond the breathing and coughing of others and the noises of the vessel and the sea — certainly no sound of guns.

Then, all at once, I picked up a threatening, faraway sound. It was a faint, endless, tireless grumbling or murmuring. I felt the sound rather than heard it; I would not lose that sound for months to come.

Fellows came up from breakfast and pressed behind us. Some would cry out and some said nothing, according to their nature. But all in all it was a sober gathering, and with good reason.

After a while the sound of firing grew more distinct, until it became a sullen, weariless booming with the power to intoxicate the heart.

We had kept a fair speed all the way, but now we slowed somewhat, as though we were ahead of time. The other transports closed in a fraction and we drew up with two ships ahead of us. We bunched together and steamed towards the menacing horizon, from where the noise of battle drifted.

At last our watching was rewarded by the sight of a barren mountainous land with steep cliffs. A number of boats lay out at sea at a point where the shore formed a headland of some prominence. Although no more than dots upon the water, it was clearly the fleet.

By now the gunfire had become threatening — a grander and more awful sound than I had ever heard. The battle came closer and closer. We must have travelled faster than I realised, for soon we saw shells shattering in vast dust clouds on the hillsides.

The solemn roll of the guns had grown into a series of thunderous explosions. Now the flashes could be seen and close in-shore battleships and transport ships could be distinguished. The water was dotted with mine-sweepers and tugs.

Well out to sea hung a yellow balloon, attached to one of the tugs, used for "spotting" [aerial observation].

At first we seemed to be steering into the centre of the battle, but then it was evident that we would pass further to the left. We were drawn into a medley of small craft whose duty was over and now waited on the outskirts of the fray. Farthest of all from danger was the big yellow balloon. When we came almost underneath it I stared up, envying the observer with his telescope.

From the deck I could see very little. The land did not seem far off, and yet it must have been miles away. I could make out nothing beyond the outline of the battleships and the great shell bursts on the ridges. There was no sign of men or targets. The gun flashes, the smoke clouds and the voices of the explosions were endless and very distinct. For some time our speed had lessened a great deal, but even so we made good headway. Soon the noise of battle fell behind. The gunfire died into an endless roll and once again we were left listening.

The coast ran on and on along our starboard side, all the way the same mountainous, barren land.

The morning turned out more gloomy than it had promised. There were some patches of sunshine between the clouds and a dullness along the horizon, hinting at rain later on. We slowed down and seemed to just drift forward.

And then the trumpeter blew "Stables" once more. Nobody showed readiness to go below and sweat among the horses, but we had no choice. Before long we were jostling one another down the companion ladder, rolling out the mats and exercising the horses. The hatches of the hold were open, because men were down below fusing shells and loading up the wagons. It cramped us for room more than ever, adding risk into the bargain.

As morning wore on, the rumble of guns came down to us once more. Every minute brought the sounds with greater distinctness, until they broke into many separate explosions.

Three or four of our fellows were on deck, hauling up — by rope — the baskets of manure as fast as we filled them. I would have liked to run up the ladder and find out what was going on, but Mr Gardiner stood guard at the bottom, so I resigned myself to follow the weary procession of men and horses.

All of a sudden there was no reply to our oaths and tugging at the rope. At last a man went up to find out what was the matter. He disappeared for three or four minutes and then the whole party turned up suddenly to look through the hatch and exclaim, "There's a bonzer affair ahead."

Several men stopped what they were doing and sneaked away. In a few minutes' time Gardiner went off, leaving us alone. After that I decided to have a look as well, putting the horse I was exercising back into his stall.

When I stepped on deck a good many fellows were there already, all staring ahead. This time we were closer to land, and the vegetation could be made out. More craft seemed to be engaged or standing by. Although we were still several miles removed from the action, we saw shell bursts splashing about on the hills.

I could not stay long — Gardiner might reappear at any moment — so I dodged back again and took out the next horse. But I need not have hurried. Gardiner was nowhere near and most of the other fellows were gone. Finally, they straggled back one by one, talking with animation, laughing and calling out. We passed the news to the people sitting on the shells in the bowels of the ship. Before we had finished, Gardiner turned up again, so we had to continue exercising the horses.

For the next hour the gunfire grew more distinct, until it was obvious the fight must be near at hand. In spite of, or perhaps because of, the general unrest of the Staff, every horse received a full share of exercise, and towards midday there were still half a dozen animals to be taken out.

However, in my view I had done enough for one day. I edged behind the feed bin and at the first opportunity went up the gangway to see what was going on. Somehow or other we had drifted right into the thick of battle. We were lying two or three miles off shore, though it looked no distance over the water. The mountains seemed to run right down to the water's edge and were covered with vegetation as closely as hairs sprout on a man's head. Several big valleys ran into and over those hills. I was not particularly smitten by what I saw. It looked like an uncharitable land for an attack, a battlefield that favoured the enemy more than us.

Beside us the water teemed with boats, a Noah's Ark of boats — two of every build. There were dreadnoughts, rowing boats and everything else in between. Our place was among other transports and non-fighting craft, though there were a couple of destroyers, panting to go into action. Smoke wisps curled from their funnels, men were at their posts on deck and there was an officer at the bridge with glasses clapped to his eyes.

The armoured boats were at work, some lying miles off their targets. At short and uneven intervals one or other would send out long spouts of flame from her turrets. Over the water followed a rumble, boom or bellow, according to the size of gun or its distance. From time to time three or four funnels of dust would go up on the hilltops. Some of the targets were over ridges beyond our sight, but frequently shells fell on this side of the dull green crests. I was sure that many tragedies were happening over there, but across the stretch of water none of it could be seen — it looked calm and empty.

There seemed no proper order of firing; it was one boat here and another there. The explosions were not as continuous as earlier in the morning, which made me wonder if the crisis had passed. At first it seemed we were having it our way. Then a destroyer, only a few cable lengths away from us, had a waterspout over her bows. She retreated rather than wait for the Turkish gunner to correct his range. Our fellows were as eager as at a football final. They laughed whenever the Turks missed and called out when a bull's-eye was nearly scored.

Worried about the horses, I went down below again. The work was nearly over; men were putting back the last animals and mixing the feed for them.

Soon after that came the order, "Turn out."

By now the sun was bright and hot. I went onto the top deck and found Hawkins and one or two others there. We sat on a hatch top, watching and listening to the battle. It was Sunday, but instead of church bells, we heard the clang of twelve-inch guns. One of the party, who had a pair of binoculars, picked up a company of our infantry in the scrub on top of the hills. I thought he probably lied, for at first I saw nothing, but the truth was soon revealed. On a patch of open land a number of puny figures appeared, while our shells dropped ahead of them with precision. They crowded the open space in quick time before the scrub engulfed them. There was no sign of the enemy, who may have retreated. As the scrub told no tales, nothing more could be seen.

The battleships continued to range shells onto the hilltops in a busy manner; the enemy continued to answer. Once or twice our ship *Hindoo* seemed to be a target. A good many of us were wondering where the next shell would fall, but none came aboard. We went on yarning and watching and calculating until the bugle for "Cookhouse" sounded.

Corporal Tank had spent the morning flag-wagging on the bridge, and now he sat on the boards dangling his legs and looking at the battle. I went up and gave him a "Hullo".

"Well, what do you think?" I asked.

Tank screwed up his mouth and shrugged his shoulders.

I looked into his face and half in earnest and half jokingly I said, "Yes, later tonight a Tank or a Lake may lie spreadeagled over there."

He answered quite seriously in his funny, jerky way, "Lake, I'm not coming back . . . I saw it all quite plainly as though in a dream . . . We went over in a barge and got to shore . . . I was running up the beach, was hit and fell back . . . I saw it as plain as anything."

He was so serious he made me grin. "Sorry to hear the news, Corporal," I said. "You didn't see me there by any chance, did you?"

He looked at me in his sad way and I could not help feeling sorry for him. Tank had liver problems and consequently got the blues. I was concerned for him, so I said something reassuring before leaving.

Thinking of Tank's liver reminded me that the bugle for "Cookhouse" had gone and I would go hungry unless I hurried. I went down to the mess deck, which hummed with life from end to end. Some ate at top speed, stretching over the tables for what they wanted and shovelling food into their mouths. Others sat on the steam pipes round the room, putting together kits or cleaning rifles. A few men hung out of portholes and gave bulletins of the day.

I made a good dinner, as the first boat would leave in a couple of hours and this was our final meal on board. After the meal I dumped my kit in a corner, put the rifle with it and went on deck again.

The boat now seemed fuller than usual — everywhere were crowds, and there was no space to spare. The troop deck overflowed with men and one had to manoeuvre through the crowd. Men exclaimed and pointed whenever a shell dropped close to our ship. Though still excited by the thought of battle, on the whole the throng was a great deal quieter than it had been.

CHAPTER
FIVE

THE LANDING AT ANZAC COVE

It was not long before Mr Gardiner ordered those members of the Brigade Staff designated for landing to get into marching order. I buckled on a water bottle and haversack and hung the iron rations at my belt. There were a dozen other heavy things about me too, and when I had pulled an overcoat over my shoulder and taken hold of a rifle I felt more like sinking into an armchair than engaging an enemy.

One or two of our fellows were on the parade deck ready for a final yarn. It appeared that we were not due to leave for another two hours, so I took off my coat again and sat down. The crowding and bustling went on and the final hour came very fast.

An empty barge was brought alongside the *Hindoo* and secured with hawsers. A rope ladder was thrown over and men went down and busied themselves making ready to lower the guns and limbers with more energy than usual.

Norris had come onto the scene overloaded, like me. On his back was a box with a red cross on the lid. Both of us had to board the very first barge. Norris came up to me where I stood craning over the side, and we watched the lowering of the guns and wagons.

Then an officer turned up and ordered us to go aboard the barge at once. I gathered my kit together and with Norris pushed through the crowd to the rope ladder. There were more people than ever here; the barge bobbed up and down, making the lowering of the guns more difficult. Orders and oaths could be heard all round.

The drop down to the barge was about thirty feet and the rope ladder was not the easiest of stairways. I climbed over the rails and got hold of the ladder, praying that Norris would not fall onto my head. I felt about as nimble as a steamroller and glanced uneasily down to the people and guns below. The further I went, the more the ladder swayed, but in the end I managed to stow myself into a corner of the barge. She was broad and stout and seemed safe from shipwreck, but she lifted up and down on the choppy sea like a playful elephant.

Finally the loading was over. Three or four perspiring men knelt among the gun wheels. After making the final lashings they straightened their backs and went up the ladder.

The other fellows on the Brigade Staff had gone down to the stables, and now and then someone poked his head through the portholes. Witty remarks and jokes passed between us until the colonel and his adjutant appeared above us and started to descend the ladder; once they were aboard they made room for themselves beside me. We had A Battery guns aboard and A

Battery fellows with them. The only man still missing was the doctor.

There had been plenty of sunshine through the day, but now the weather looked uncertain. White and grey clouds chased across the blue sky and little gusts of wind got up. I hoped the evening would prove charitable, having no fancy to be drenched with rain.

We sat and waited for the doctor. A naval launch, with a junior lieutenant in charge, steamed out of nowhere towards us. He ran the launch alongside and called out in high-pitched tones asking us if we were ready. He was a big, fat fellow and very much at ease. No doubt he had run the vessel to the shore several times already.

A hawser was cast aboard our barge and we fastened ourselves to the launch.

The overweight lieutenant repeated, "Are you ready, sir?"

"No," the colonel shouted back. "The doctor is still not here! Where's that Doc?" he exclaimed impatiently, more to himself than anyone else. "What's the matter with the fellow?"

Just then the doctor showed up above and the colonel, who had cast a hundred glances that way during the last five minutes, shouted out, "Hurry up, Doc — hurry up, man! You're late!"

The doctor came down the ladder as fast as he could and half a dozen hands steadied him for the final drop. He was barely aboard when the naval officer called out again, "If you're ready, sir, cast off from the ship, please!"

We threw our ropes overboard and the launch moved up ahead of us, straining on the hawser, and taking us in tow. Now we were moving gently through the water with the great hull of the ship towering above us. In their hundreds the remaining fellows on the ship hung over the side and sent after us their best luck. Corporal Woods's dark head looked through a porthole and wished us good luck. I felt he envied me my seat in the barge.

Then we were free from the ship and speeding briskly along. We were clear of other craft when we turned our course towards the hills.

Now we passed into clearer waters and choppy waves splashed our sides, sending the clumsy barge bumping up and down. The officers and fellows sat quietly in their places, looking at the land, which was growing in size and shape. I sat as quietly as any, and my gaze too seldom left the land. The moment I had often thought about had come, and I felt myself ready for it.

Forward we went towards frowning Turkey with its looming cliffs at the slow pace of a pleasure boat heading for a picnic ground. Ten minutes, five minutes and we would meet Turkish rifle fire.

So there we sat in the horse barge, as still as could be, some shielded by the guns and wagons, some bent forward, but all of us thankful the hour had struck. In the launch, a cable's length away, every man was behind armour. The officer looked through a hole before him and turned from time to time to the man at the engine, who was frowning and looking at the land.

We throbbed over the choppy waters and the hills approached, full of ragged gullies bristling with stunted scrub. Not a soldier moved among them, not a puff of smoke came out, but there was a roar of guns behind us and a far-off bubbling sound ahead. I did not know what it meant then, but I would learn its grim meaning soon enough.

Forward we went, and the band of waters narrowed and a strip of sandy shore came out below the hills. Then high overhead passed a thin, whining sound and the first bullet flicked the water, only yards away. We were within rifle range of the Turks.

"Get under cover, everyone!" somebody called out. All those who could dived down among the wagons. A second bullet went by and a third, but they passed high over us. Strangely enough, the sound did not frighten me.

We neared shore quickly — only half a mile of water intervened and the beach was now clearly visible. I was surprised to see crowds of people on that narrow strip of sand. There were stacks of stores piled everywhere and straight in front of us was a complete wireless plant, fully rigged. They had lost no time! By Jove, there were sappers[15] and a mule battery as well.

As we bumped along a few more bullets whistled our way. Those and an odd dose of shrapnel, falling far off, were all the attention the enemy gave us. But nearer to land matters warmed up.

By now steady doses of shrapnel were coming over the hills. They were meant for the beach, no doubt, but the angle of descent was tricky and nearly all of them

101

overshot the mark and hissed into the water. To hear the crack of a shell overhead and a rush of bullets on the waves made one start measuring the distance to the friendly cliffs. I crouched down between a wagon wheel and the side of the barge. Despite an uneasy feeling, I poked up my head from time to time to watch the approaching shore and mark where the last shower of bullets hit the water.

Now we were close at hand and every man rose on one knee, awaiting the order to jump ashore.

"I'm leaving you now, sir," came the naval lieutenant's English voice. "They'll land you from shore, sir!"

The launch slowed down, cast us off and backed out to sea. "Hey there," the lieutenant shouted. "Get this barge ashore!" And that was the last I saw of the launch, for her crew was as prudent as they were brave. I heard her chug-chug away for safer waters.

A party of men ran across the beach to catch our ropes and hauled us resolutely ashore. The beach shelved slowly into the water so that we scraped on the pebbles some way out. There was too much shrapnel for comfort. Soon we passed the most dangerous zone and headed for the beach.[16]

"That's as far as she'll come!" someone on the rope was calling out. "Lower the front board! The beach is all pebbles so it's hard enough. Run the guns from where you are!"

Our fellows were already at the chains holding up the front of the barge.

The board went down with a splash and the gunners started to roll out the first gun. I jumped onto the side of the barge and worked my way forward as fast as I could. The colonel and adjutant scrambled ashore. The sergeant-major stood in the water, supervising the unloading of the gun. He fell on his back into the water when the gun accidentally ran into him. I thought it was the end of him, but he emerged again.

There was no time for gazing, though, as Colonel Jackson had vanished into the crowd and I had to find him. Through the water I went, then splashed onto the beach and chased after the colonel over the shingle. Not far away I caught up with him; he was talking to Colonel Irons, who was frowning and answering in an impatient way. I kept Colonel Jackson in the corner of my eye while I looked around. I was jumpy, for the beach was entirely without cover, and who knew when a shell would burst and come tearing over in our direction?

Men moved about me with haste and purpose. The loudest noise was the buzzing of the wireless plant, which spelt out its messages at racing speed.

Then my eye fell on the first dead soldier. He lay on his back where the waves moved up and down across the sand, so that part of him was soaking wet and part quite dry. His fingers were stiff and spread out, his flesh was mottled and his mouth smiled a vacant smile. Doubtless somewhere at home a wife or mother prayed for his safekeeping.[17]

There seemed no regimental order here. Men of all corps milled about and officers were as numerous as privates. Nobody shot at anything, none flourished swords, there was not an enemy to be discovered. The place was more like the waiting room of a station, a bank or government office, where everyone is going somewhere and nobody is getting anywhere.

The advance party had left enduring marks. Two newly dug roads started off into the interior; a gigantic stack of provisions was growing a few yards from the waterline and barges dumped quantities of small arms and ammunition on the sand.

On the side of the hills many a man was digging his first funkhole.[18] The anchorage was not a whit less busy than the beach. Infantry reinforcements came in steadily, ammunition barges and provision boats approached or lay at anchor close in-shore. Pinnaces and rowing boats dodged round and round one another. Under a Red Cross flag, flapping in the breeze, lay line upon line of stretchers with their mangled loads. While the orderlies were busy with the bandages, fresh cases kept arriving.

The two colonels talked on for some time: Colonel Irons vigorous and impatient, like a man much put out, and our colonel quiet as always, lifting his eyebrows and pursing his mouth now and again. The conversation between them ended suddenly. Then Colonel Jackson turned round and strode over in my direction. I could see he was annoyed. He made me no sign, but went past me towards our barge. I followed him, and soon after we ran into the adjutant waiting there. "The guns must go back!" the colonel began abruptly . . . that was all I heard.[19]

Later on I was told we were under fire from the Turks and retreating fast. Apparently, General Birdwood believed that the position was untenable and must be given up at night. This may have been the truth or not — there were many liars creating disturbing rumours on that beach that day.[20]

"You come with me, Lake," Colonel Jackson said, and with that he started over the pebbles in the direction we had first taken.

In certain places there were as many sailors as soldiers, for the British Navy was in charge of the landing. Some of these British sailors were in khaki dress, and although they were a scratch lot, they worked well.

Beside a stock of ammunition were two little midshipmen or naval cadets, guarding it like two bantam cocks. They were no age at all and must have gone to some trouble to get there, both believing themselves protected by a revolver at their belt. This way and that way they bobbed, like sparrows on a twig. Every time a shell clapped overhead, they giggled and dived for shelter. And next instant the jolly little fellows bobbed out again.

An elderly admiral in blue coat and white trousers wandered around — a tough customer, one of the bulldog breed. He seemed able to abuse everybody, soldiers and sailors alike. There was always a heartier pull on a rope whenever he looked that way.

Hampered by the crowd, the shingle beach and the weight of my equipment, it was hard to keep up with

105

the colonel, who went over the beach in long strides as if out of temper with the whole affair.

We came to a place where a deep ravine ran into the hills. In winter the bottom of the ravine was probably a watercourse, but now in spring it was dry. The banks, densely covered with scrub, were very steep, and they narrowed as we advanced, so it gave us some shelter from shrapnel. The headquarters of several units had found this out and taken refuge here.

We went along the gully, which kept a straight course and climbed all the way. We passed several dugouts, all of which were occupied, and eventually arrived at the Divisional Artillery Headquarters. All the fellows were there, crowding as close to the right bank as possible. A stream of shrapnel clapped over our heads and fell in the bushes nearby, but we were fairly secure, especially when sitting down.

Divisional Artillery had reserved two dugouts, which were large enough to accommodate us. One was just above the other. The officers occupied the top one and we men the other. A colonel and adjutant from the Indian Army shared the space with our officers.

Colonel Jackson left a few minutes later and went back to the beach, but he told me to stay where I was.

Later in the afternoon it became overcast and a drizzle of rain set in. The place became very depressing. The officers put on their coats and talked among themselves in a cheerless way. One even went to sleep. The fellows beside me had come over in the early morning and were full of rumours, but none had any reliable news to impart. They claimed that we had captured countless guns and had driven the Turks across the Peninsula and the battle was almost over. But their stories were not very credible. But one thing was certain — that all day endless numbers of wounded had arrived from the firing line.

I unrolled my coat and put it on. The drizzle continued and shadows of late afternoon darkened the scene. The leaves grew heavy with moisture and started to drip into our dugouts. The ground of the dusty watercourse became wet and looked like turning our camping site into a treacherous area. For safety's sake we huddled close against the bank and spoke little. The drip of the leaves had a tricky way of creeping under the collar of my coat. I wished the colonel would return and take me with him to a more comfortable place.

Eventually the drizzle cleared, and low in the sky the sun came out in a watery fashion. For supper we had nothing other than those tough square biscuits given to us as rations — they were so hard a man could break his teeth on them. I had three days' provisions with me, but was warned that they might have to last for five days. So I took care not to dip too deeply into my provision bag. Someone offered me the bottom of a can of tea, which helped to wash those tough biscuits down.

The guns at sea had shut their mouths, but the bubbling noise of rifle fire continued endlessly. The enemy never tired of shelling the beach, and time after time shells came tearing over our way, but they would have found it difficult to touch us where we were, although the rifle bullets kept us close to the wall.

It was said that the place was peopled with snipers, which seemed possible, as the dense bushes and scrub could conceal a whole battalion of them. One could find comfort in knowing that the enemy was little better off than we, yet to look over this ocean of bushes with its lurking army gave a sense of unease.

The Indian colonel sat down on a rock, and a native orderly took off his boots and gently massaged his feet. He appeared to have had a hard day, and his face was yellow and seamed.

Finally Colonel Jackson turned up in the adjacent dugout, drank some tea and started an earnest talk with Colonel Irons. I tried to read something from their faces, but ended up no wiser than before.

"Lake," the colonel called out. I went over gladly enough. Adjutant Yards was getting ready to leave and I was assigned to follow him. We picked our road down the watercourse. Wherever a bit of extra shelter was offered by the banks we came upon groups of officers and men, forcing us to step with care over them.

We saw small groups of men poring over maps and talking in low tones; others sat back in gloomy contemplation. In one or two cases men were eating a meagre meal.

It was not long before we arrived at the open beach. After his fashion, Adjutant Yards never said a word. He paused and looked about him for a few moments, then we turned left, keeping as near to the base of the hills as we could.

The sun was setting and streams of angry yellow light filled the western part of the sky. It was still light, but very soon evening would come. The battleships had given up their bombardments, but nowhere else were there signs of relaxation. Evening haze loomed over a sea on which countless craft were still on the go, and the beach was still crowded with men.

We continued on solid ground — the shifting pebbles scarcely reached to here. We passed our original landing place and went on until another ravine in the hills opened before us. Where we now stood the sappers had formed the beginnings of a road. Further along they had cut steps up another steep slope. Enemy shrapnel was coming over very briskly, but all of it burst higher up. We stood there for a little while as we had done at the last gully mouth.

Yards looked up and down the hill to see whether it corresponded with the directions given to him. Then we went up the gully and soon ascended a sharp rise. At the summit we went round a small shoulder on the hill, and all at once we were right on top of an A Battery gun in action.

With all cover behind us we proceeded to the gun and sat down a little to one side of it. There was no cover for anybody and the shrapnel arrived fast and very close. To speak the truth, I found myself pretty jumpy. Yet it would have needed a handsome cheque to sell my seat to anyone. We were in a kind of natural cup between two small hills. I sat stock still while our men fired the last four shells — only Heaven knew what their target was.

The climax of the sunset arrived — one portion of the sky was angry yellow and red and the remainder full of sullen moving clouds, which made the evening cheerless. There was still enough light to see some distance with ease, so we could clearly pick out the faces of the gunners and make out what they did.

Apparently we had made ourselves unpopular, because the enemy searched for us and the spot became most unhealthy. Turkish shrapnel came tearing over our way in the most unpleasant manner and often three or four puffs of smoke sailed over us at one moment. The shells burst a short distance to our right, against the fiery sunset. Once the sun had faded and darkness set in, the enemy ceased firing.

Yards got up when Major Felix came over. I heard a little of what was said and gathered that we had engaged an enemy gun; the major believed he had silenced it. While they continued talking I watched the sky and the sea and witnessed how the land dissolved into dark shadows. I listened to the fierce roll of rifle fire, now very near. When Yards came over my way I rose and followed him down to the beach.

When we came back it was dark in the gully. The sky had clouded over again and very few stars showed. The drizzling rain had resumed in drifts that came and went. Everything was damp and forbidding. Our camp was cramped and rough, but without doubt it was the safest spot anywhere around.

Adjutant Yards sat higher up with the officers. Several men were turning in for the night, lying down fully dressed with only their boots off. Their bed consisted of one blanket and an overcoat. Lying down left us more pressed for room than ever, as nobody was willing to

110

leave the immediate shelter of the bank. Coming last, I had to look for my own spot, which I found some yards lower down the watercourse. The place was full of stones and rather exposed. I moved as close as possible under the bank and removed the largest stones. At uncertain intervals they were shelling us again. The shells burst overhead with a blinding red flash, as though they were pictures of fireworks in a storybook.

I took my boots off, made the regulation bed of a blanket and overcoat and huddled myself up in it. The night was not cold and we were well screened from wind, but the depressing drizzle managed to find a way everywhere. Occasionally a few stars stared down, but they hid themselves very quickly again. In a dazed way I looked at the stars as they were coming and going. Although I had done no heavy work that day, I was glad to be lying down.

Now and then I saw the bushes moving, whether from the wind or from gathering raindrops. At times I would have vowed I'd seen moving bodies behind the bushes — was it imagination or were there snipers? I lay awake for a long time, watching and listening anxiously. I woke and slept, woke and slept. Twice the rain pattered in my face, forcing me to cover my head. Once the colonel went away, giving me his field glasses, his map-case and other things to look after. Then men on guard relieved one another and trod on me in the process.

Yet again I was wakened, this time by two fellows lying not far from me who were speaking in muted tones. "There's a bloke moving in the bushes. I heard something for sure. Is anybody round the other side?"

"I don't think so."

"Could be a sniper."

The other fellow grunted. "We'd better make certain." He stood up, went a little way into the bushes and poked about with his bayonet. The search was without result, so he came back and lay down again.

I was just dozing off again when a couple of bullets plonked into the bank three or four feet overhead and showers of dirt trickled down. I woke up with a vengeance and pondered where else I could go. In the end I dragged everything another few yards lower down, where I was alone and could be even closer to the right bank. I felt more secure, but was wide awake and stayed so for a long time.

CHAPTER
SIX

"DIG, DIG, DIG, UNTIL YOU ARE SAFE"

GENERAL SIR IAN HAMILTON, COMMANDER-IN-CHIEF TO GENERAL BIRDWOOD

I got up feeling like a cat rubbed the wrong way. I could not take my clothes off and there was nowhere to wash other than the sea. We breakfasted on hardtack biscuits and bully beef, washed down with a mouthful of water. Afterwards I sat huddled and yawning, lacking a toothbrush and picking my teeth with a twig from the nearest bush. It was pretty cold and I wished the colonel would make a start on his travels. He arrived when breakfast was over and we set off for the beach, which was just as crowded and busy as the previous day.[21]

There was now more ammunition about and a larger stack of provisions. Our battleships were moving and Turkish shrapnel came over in bursts. We spent much time on the beach and saw the sun rising in the sky. We went this way, that way and every way, tramping over the shingle and threading our way through the crowd.

The colonel met endless officers, talked plans with some and gave orders to those who had just arrived ashore.

The morning was bright with sunshine, the air a trifle sharp. Over the ocean climbed thin smoke lines from the battleships and transports. High up into the sky they went, for there was no wind to speak of. Between those waiting giants and the shore hurried the thousand small craft we had seen yesterday.

We came upon a party of sailors leaning back on a rope lashed to a barge. The group was large and a warrant officer with a gold band on his sleeve took charge. The men were elderly or youthful naval reservists. The raw army recruits had the pinched, pallid faces that London breeds.

Their warrant officer was short and vast of girth; a khaki sun hat covered a face seamed and red from tropical sun and strong spirits. He looked like a barrel on legs. I guess his wife made small demur when he packed up for the wars.

The officer marched solemnly up and down the line of men, eyeing this one and that one and giving short, sharp commands. Meanwhile, the shrapnel continued to lob over, sometimes clawing at the water and at other times spurting onto the pebbles. I could not help measuring the distance to the friendly cliffs, though retreating would be unfavourably considered, so I swelled out my chest and tried to look as though I was enjoying it.

Now the men on the rope pulled away, some with an even haul and some in a jerky fashion, for their minds were on the shells hurling over. Some dropped down onto the ground and grinned in a sheepish and unhappy manner. Suddenly there was a rush and a bang right over our heads and that poor line of Cockneys crouched this way and that. One fellow dropped the rope, ran away and hid under the cliff. The portly warrant officer turned round and roared out, "Come out of that, you skulker! If you be killed, you be killed. If you run you'll be shot anyway!" Shamed in front of his comrades the man came back — the rope straightened again and the barge came ashore at last.

Finally the colonel's business on the beach ended and we went the way I had gone the previous night. The sappers had finished making the road, which now wound out of sight over the hill.

We followed the ravine and I assumed we were about to look for the A Battery gun. However, we moved to the right and gained the crest that way. I say "gained the crest", but we stopped short of the top, for on the other side a battle was raging. Had all been quiet one would have looked and beheld only the wilderness, as the guns were hidden in clumps of scrub and of the infantry there was no sign. Later I found a few of them in a trench behind the guns, quite close to us. I wondered what they were doing there.

Now the sun had climbed up into the sky — a warming sun that left the scrubland silvery and quivering and threw a haze over the open country. A great breast of a cliff, which we called Achi Baba, rose up beyond a broad plain. In front of us were hills and valleys and behind us the glass-flat sea.

We stayed there only briefly, as a bullet slammed by and set us thinking of healthier places. On the right of the crest was a scooped-out spot, probably some old

115

Turkish observation post. It was just what the colonel was looking for. We jumped down into the dugout and dropped onto our knees. It had a depth of three or four feet, so we could stay protected while looking over the top, scanning the whole countryside.

The morning was wonderfully pretty — the place was all browns and smoky blues and ablaze with sunlight.

The rifle fire rolled from all around and the hissing bursts of machine guns were born and died. There was the plucky "bang-bang" of a mountain battery and the heavier voice of our own gun. But the roar of battle was less hideous here, as the bellowing from the guns at sea could not be heard.

I was on my knees with only my head above the parapet, not an inch more than need be. The firing came from all over the place, so much so that it was hard to tell which was from us and which from the enemy. The battle went on briskly, but it had to wait for my attention. I was busy roaming a farmer's eye across that charming landscape full of contrast.

The colonel and I were perched in a land that in happier days may have grazed flocks of Turkish sheep and goats. Over in the distance was a wide flat country of vines and cropland, even now filling with the harvest. Humble homes were hidden there, with anxious wives or aged mothers as guardians, while sons and husbands had gone forth, changing a sickle for a rifle.

Somewhere in that flat country the enemy lay, though I could not spot them without field glasses. I gradually discovered our own men beneath us, somewhat to the left. A mountain gun and our own A Battery gun were no more than a few hundred yards away. Yet one had to look keenly to see our green-uniformed gunners or the Indians in their khaki puggarees. Only their movements and the flashes of their guns made it possible to detect them.

There was an old trench behind the guns, filled with a number of our infantry. It had little depth, and from up here one could look right in. The fellows crouched or sat, rifle in hand, but giving no assistance to the assault. I could not understand how such a position had been chosen for an attack.

A track ran round the shoulder of our hill, joining the beach with a broad valley that thrust into the mountains. One could not follow the course of the valley far, as hills interrupted. I believed that at its head lay the trenches our infantry held. The track curved in front of the guns and was exposed all the way to the enemy. Yet continually people passed up and down that track, many of them wounded.

There were lonely infantrymen, who came out of the valley and disappeared towards the beach. There were those who passed at a walking pace and those who went by at a halting run, trying to dodge the guns. Several lines of stretcher cases passed at a slow pace down the road, and walking wounded appeared, leaning on the shoulders of friends. Everyone who came from the battlegrounds was covered in dust, parched and tired. Some men returned towards the valley; most of them were stretcher-bearers. Some ran as fast as their weary limbs allowed, but others plodded forward

117

slowly, being wounded, worn out or stunned by the continuous shelling.[22]

Of all those who passed, I remember best an Army chaplain supporting a wounded man. They approached with the utmost slowness from the valley. The chaplain was engrossed in his task, and the wounded man was beyond caring what befell him. I watched them all the way, stunned by their slowness and lack of concern at the hubbub around them as they stumbled along the path towards the medical post on the beach.

Meanwhile, fierce shelling continued. Officers came up beside us, talked a little with the colonel, looked around, then went away again. One who came was Major Andrews; I overheard that we were landing more guns. Some of the Brigade Staff were on their way over and the major spoke of meeting them.

All the while the colonel said never a word to me, but scanned the field with his glasses and once or twice used a telescope. Often he would look towards the beach and curse the delay in getting the additional guns.

This cup in the hills was not the only spot surrounded by battle. The enemy still targeted the beach and the sea, and many shells went whistling past us over that way. I would have welcomed a move, but just then I caught sight of some Brigade Staff members climbing up from the beach. They had just landed and had field telephones and other equipment with them. The new arrivals panted from their efforts to climb to the rise just below us.

The colonel leaned over the parapet, exposing himself to great danger. He called out impatiently to Lieutenant Gardiner, the officer in charge of the guns. "What about the guns, Mr Gardiner? What have you done with them?"

"They're here, sir. We met up with the major!"

During the explanations it became clear that the guns were going the wrong way. After Gardiner was sharply corrected he went back in a hurry.

Though things straightened out, the morning was full of confusion and running about. The afternoon was no better. Until evening I followed close on the colonel's heels while he went this way, that way and every way. Endlessly we walked over pebbles and up and down the lower hills near the beach. All day enemy shells came from every angle, tumbling about us or violently tearing up the waters. All day the transports brought reinforcements: barges full of ammunition, provisions and guns.

Men dug in wherever an inch of cover could be found. Toiling lines of men dragged field guns from the beach along the roads to positions on the hills. Every hour left us surer of our footing, but it did not prevent more and more of us being killed. Hospital ships loaded with wounded sailed away and others steamed in from the far horizon to collect the next load of injured men.[23]

By night we artillery fellows had made our headquarters near the battlefield of that morning. When the colonel and I came back, men were digging in the guns. It was necessary to keep communicating all

119

through the night with Divisional Artillery by means of lamp signals. The Staff were taking turns at this. My turn was scheduled for the middle of the night.

Communications were still chaotic. Many men were missing, presumed killed. High above us were heaped piles of dead and maimed men, who had stood their trial and proven themselves under fire.

I dug a shallow hole, and when the stars came out, took off my boots and lay down. The bad weather had cleared away and the stars were very bright. And so the second day ended. Once more darkness covered up the ruins and the agony.

When I was small, Grandmother Lake used to take me onto her knee and ask me to pray for the welfare of the British and Indian armies. At that time her husband was a colonel in the Indian Army. I wondered whether Granny Lake had gone to Valhalla, the Hall of the Gods, and whether she was waiting there for the arrival of her grandson, who had in the end followed family tradition and gone to war.

Hardly was I asleep when someone shook me by the shoulder. I opened my eyes to find the stars shining. Wilkinson was kneeling beside me.

"What's the time?" I mumbled.

"Twelve o'clock and it's your shift."

I muttered, yawned and sat up. "What's to be done?"

"Watch Divisional Artillery for lamp signals. Do an hour on watch then wake Foster. He's next man."

I nodded and yawned again. Wilkinson disappeared.

With many an unuttered curse I got to my feet. A keen wind had risen, so I put my coat on and turned up the collar over my head and neck. Then I put on my big woollen cap, thanking a good lady from Melbourne who had knitted it.

I stumbled along the track to a better spot and sat down. The stars shone clearly, but the sea, the hillsides and the beach were folded in gloom. Distant rifle fire sounded incessantly, like the boiling of a pot. Every few minutes a shell whistled overhead and burst with menace in the sea.

The transports lay several miles away, the battleships lay in front of them, and destroyers moved restlessly in and out. Numerous other craft of every kind were there, anchored among the shadows closer in to shore. I saw the Morse lamps winking at each other and felt companionship, knowing others watched with me. My eyes followed the great yellow searchlights in their ceaseless journey round the bay and knew that others also guarded the sleeping multitude.

Soon I stood up. The wind stirred the low bushes perpetually. My mind was still weary with the events of the previous day. Once again I saw dead men and torn beasts in their death struggles and heard the guns that had killed them. At this solemn hour the sacrifice and the struggle seemed useless.

Presently the night air crept through my coat and sent my hands into pockets and myself moving up and down. For all my watching, no signal appeared; instead my footsteps on the path sounded mournfully. An army

121

slept in the ragged scrub on either side of me. Finally, to lose my thoughts, I put together a battle prayer.

> Trench by trench, along the line,
> Dies the spluttering musketry;
> And the gunners at their guns
> Lay the heavy shrapnel by,
> God of Battle! God of Right!
> Guard and guide Thy troops this night!
> Here and here, among the hills,
> Gleam the tiny supper fires;
> There and there a hard-spent man
> To a barren bed retires.
> Now across the darkened bowl,
> Pass the stars on their patrol,
> Staring down on War's still feast,
> Mangled man and broken beast,
> God of Battle! God of Right!
> Guard and guide Thy troops this night!

Steps and voices were approaching behind me. Instantly I woke up and drew into deeper shadow. I stood there for several moments, while the shuffling steps advanced. They proved to be a stretcher party, arriving at a painfully slow pace round the bend in the path. With much tenderness the Red Cross men carried their burdens past me. I left the path altogether for them to file by — a sorrowful, halting procession. One soldier was lying on a stretcher with a torn shoulder, another one with a bloody bandage wrapped around his face and yet another with shattered legs that would never walk again. The stretcher-bearers went by in gloom and silence, with their eyes cast down and with grey faces.

After them shambled a large crowd of soldiers with bandaged arms and legs. They talked in low tones, some of them smoking cigarettes.

I heard a voice say, "Don't think much of these smokes, but you'll take anything here."

A gruffer voice replied, "Blasted bad luck getting put out of action on the second day. You know Corporal Davis, that big bouncing brute in D Company? He got a bullet through his heart, poor sod. 'E jumped about ten foot in the air when it happened."

And then a third voice: "I've got three in the arm from that swine of a machine gun. It's aching like hell!" And so the column of wounded passed on their way to the Red Cross station on the beach.

My hour was up and the watch over. Gladly I hurried off and pulled my relief out of bed. Next minute the blankets were over me and I fell asleep.

It was dawn when I woke. I opened one eye, then the other, then took courage and propped myself on one elbow. Already the beach showed life and movement and our battleships were taking up new stations at sea. Nobody nearby seemed awake; the bushes looked empty and mysterious. Far away the everlasting rifle fire went on, dying, growing and dying away again.

From that painful bed, cut out of the hillside, I watched morning growing out of the night. The curves among the hills took shape, the waters moved into life

123

and in the distance rose the faint peaks of the island of Imbros.

Once again I found the bay filled with vessels of all size.[24] Cruisers and battleships manoeuvred from point to point. Scouts and destroyers sped along a thoroughfare where mine-sweepers, trawlers, tugboats, colliers, barges, pontoons, lifeboats and rowing boats jostled one another. The transports rode beyond them with thin smoke lines creeping to the sky, and with them waited the hospital ships for the burden the day would bring. I watched till morning broke. Then I threw aside the blanket, sat up and put out a hand for my boots.

The beach soon resembled a marketplace. Men in groups or singly hurried this way and that — Red Cross men bore wounded on stretchers, Indians led mules, sailors in parties hauled ashore guns and limbers, artillery men loaded themselves with ammunition, infantrymen lined up to receive spades and then returned to the trenches they were digging. Greeks stabled donkeys, men stacked piles of bully beef and tins of biscuits. Guns and limbers blocked the way, lines of wounded lay sheltered beneath the cliffs.

Further on men were gathering vast stores of provisions, and tanks for fresh water stood where the waves lapped the pebbles. Sacks of flour were thrown into growing heaps beside sacks of sugar. Cases of tea were dumped on the sand. Cheeses and sides of bacon were arriving. Sheets of tin roofing lay in piles, waiting for the shins of the unwary.

Some men loaded lengths of wood and others staggered under bales of hay. Gangs of sappers made roads along the hillsides and telephonists ran wires from bush to bush. Infantry parties carried sandbags on their heads going towards the firing line and others trudged uphill, loaded with water bottles. Men mooched round with rifles on their backs and men were there with picks and shovels, digging, digging, digging![25] The murmurs of life rose up like a mighty ocean tide.

The hillside awoke and became peopled with men drawing on shirts and pulling at boots. Blue and khaki blankets appeared on half the bushes, waiting for the tardy sun. Later, wisps of smoke curled up from fifty different places.

Already our gunners were lingering around their guns, placing the last sandbags along the parapets and stacking the ammunition brought by men toiling up the hill. The guns were lowered nearly to ground level, protected by heavy ramparts of earth and sandbags and camouflaged with leafy boughs. I was surprised by how much had been done while I slept.

Access trenches ran out from the gun positions and telephone wires linked them up with the observing station. The funk-holes for the gunners ran alongside the guns.

Now at last, as if reluctant, the sun got up. First I could only see her beams come creeping round the corner, which made the bushland warm and cheerful while the damp fled away from patches of brown earth. Insects came out from cracks and crevices and set about finding us. The birds made love in the greenery, puffing their breasts out and chirruping with morning confidence.

The cook had boiled some tea and fried rashers of bacon. He sent me a "Cooee" and I went over with a mess tin. There were half a dozen men around the fire holding out tin pannikins for filling. Hawkins was crouched among the ashes, stirring an evil-looking mess meant to be Welsh rarebit. He was too interested to look up, but the others greeted me with, "How are things?" I did not feel talkative, and answered with a noncommittal nod.

There were two rashers of bacon each and as many biscuits as a man wanted. I went back to my funk-hole, balancing biscuits and bacon in one hand and a pot of tea in the other.

Just then the yellow observation balloon went up.

I had grown so used to the perpetual rifle fire that I no longer heard it. Though the enemy still shelled us, it was in a casual manner, and they were overshooting the mark, so most of their endeavours ended in the sea. Sometimes a hail of bullets descended on the beach with a whizz and a bang, and some poor fellow would fall over fatally wounded, and maybe two or three others would hobble away; but this happened very seldom.

Then I noticed one of the battleships draw to a standstill and swing about. I was just pouring the pannikin of tea down my throat when she vomited a thousand-pound shell halfway across the peninsula. As

I stopped choking, a cruiser took up the running. Another round of battle had begun.

I hurried the rest of my breakfast down and stayed within call of the observing station. The other fellows collected the flags and telephones. The usual abuse was exchanged.

"What the hell have you done with those flags? Can't you leave a blasted cove's things alone for a minute? They were there before breakfast!"

"I've not touched your damned things. You'll need a bloody nursemaid!"

The colonel, the adjutant, the sergeant-major and Wilkinson climbed up to the Brigade observing station. Not far away and lower down, Major Felix, his sergeant-major and Eaves, the telephonist, took possession of a dugout. The B Battery observing station was higher up, to the left. The whole position was utterly congested, but nowhere else was there room.

A dozen yards below the Brigade observing station Eaves curled himself up, his head fastened to a telephone running to Divisional Artillery. I received orders to perch myself halfway between him and the observing station, under the shelter of an overhanging ledge.

CHAPTER
SEVEN

THE BIG GUNS OF HMS *QUEEN ELIZABETH*

The bombardment grew in volume as battleship after battleship engaged a target. Like a colossal thunderstorm, explosions roared around the bay. The very ground was trembling. Now the veteran HMS *Triumph* opened fire. The majestic HMS *Queen Elizabeth*, headquarters of General Hamilton and for the entire expedition, drew further out and came to a standstill.

The sun was mounting and had turned unpleasantly fierce. There was not a puff of wind and not a cloud in the sky; the blue waters of Saros were without ruffle or furrow. I became aware that the rifle fire was more intense and that machine guns were opening in sharp bursts along the lines. We, for our part, were ready now: the gunners were waiting in their funk-holes behind the guns, the section commanders were at their posts — Major Felix with the megaphone in his hand. But still no order for action came through.

The effect of the ships' fire quickly became apparent, as the enemy woke up with a vengeance. The Turks answered with salvos of shrapnel and lyddite,[26] following hard on each other's heels and coming over our heads with a rush and a bang which were unholy, to say the least.

Many of the enemy's salvos fell around the craft in the bay, but some were better timed and poured into the bushes, sending us close into whatever shelter was handy. Other deadly charges hissed onto the crowded beach, where there was a sporting chance of bagging anything from generals to tin cans. After a lucky shot a riot would start among the mules, or some poor chap would fall down and go to his Maker. Then they would cry out for stretcher-bearers and Red Cross men. Or maybe a party hauling at some gun would scatter without warning behind a pile of stores, like mice into a hole.

Long ago conversation had grown impossible, but there were moments of relative silence. Then one would hear the frantic splutter of rifle fire from the head of the valley, the distant but fierce bursts of machine guns and the barking of our little Indian mountain batteries. I could distinctly hear the loud buzz of the wireless plant telling the British Navy what targets to engage. Also at such times strange cries rose from the beach.

By now we gunners were sheltering in our funk-holes. But the road from the valley was still populous, full of long processions of wounded toiling to the Red Cross headquarters below.

An infantryman in fighting order with a haversack on his back came scrambling up the hill, found room beside me and planted himself there. He could not speak for panting and was about to break down. Fortunately, the place he secured was fairly well

129

protected and confidence came back with breath. I glanced at him as he crouched down — he was a thin, weak fellow and turned out to be a liar. I said nothing to him because he was upset and because the sun was getting too hot for talking. I went on watching the beach.

"Hullo, cobber," he said at last.

"Hullo," I answered and turned towards him.

He looked at me out of the palest of blue eyes. "I just come from the firing line," he said. "It's murder there. What are you blokes doing?"

"Going to shoot soon, I suppose," I replied.

"Gettin' any losses 'ere?"

"Most of the fire is going over, but we'll be shooting in a minute or two and that ought to open the ball in earnest."

He said nothing, and soon he got up and crept away. He passed from view, but I noted that he was not bound for the firing line.

It was going to be a hot day. I pushed my finger into the neck of my shirt, which was already clammy with perspiration. A haze had fallen over the more distant parts of the bay, and round my ears a solitary fly buzzed with persistence.

Orders came through. Near me Major Felix held a megaphone to his mouth and called out.

"Infantry advancing! Aiming point, left ridge of Battleship Hill! Line of fire, twenty degrees three-oh minutes right! Corrector one-five-oh-three-six hundred! Angle of sight three degrees one-oh minutes elevation! One round, battery FIRE!"

The section commander saluted and shouted to his sergeants, who kneeled at the trails, saluted and turned to the gunners. No. 3 on the left seat laid the gun; No. 6 set the fuse and No. 5 passed the shell to No. 4. No. 2, on the right-hand seat, opened the breech; No. 4 pushed home the shell; No. 2 closed the breech again. After a pause the command "FIRE" was given. Then followed a mighty uproar, which seemed to beat the ground and plunge back again onto my ears. The boughs near the guns sprang into the air, long tongues of flame leaped forth and the gun-barrels slid backwards and into place again.

The seconds went by.

Again Major Felix was shouting. "C gun, five minutes more left! Shorten corrector six! Drop two-oh-oh! Repeat!"

"What?" the section commander shouted.

The order came again, but louder.

The section commander saluted and turned to his sergeants, the sergeants saluted and directed the gunners, and again the uproar seemed to rebound and strike me.

A third time the order came: "C gun, two minutes more left! Drop five-oh! FIRE!"

We were into it with a vengeance now, equally engaged by land and by sea. The enemy fire never slackened for a moment — the sky became more terrible with travelling shells and more beautiful with delicate bursts of shrapnel. At intervals mighty howitzer shells rumbled solemnly through space and plunged into the sea amid columns of spray.[27] We gunners must soon have made ourselves unwelcome, for the enemy guns started to search for us, and quickly the game of hide and seek became too hot for pleasure.

I was still perched under the projecting ledge, but my time was coming. Eaves lifted up his transmitter and began to call: "Hullo, hullo!" A message was coming through from Divisional Artillery. Presently, receiver at ear, Eaves wrote it down. Next he read it through and then beckoned me. "Here you are," he said, holding out the message in his huge hand.

I took the paper and began to crawl up the bank to the observing station. Matters were livelier than ever in the open. Shells were bursting like the devils of hell, and rifle bullets went by with the slashing sound of steel on steel. The ascent was a matter of seconds. I leaned over the edge of the dugout and saw Wilkinson, telephone at ear, lying in a half-moon in his own funk-hole. In the main dugout sat the colonel, the adjutant and the sergeant-major, with maps across their knees.

An argument was going on. News had come through that we were shelling our own infantry.

"They're dirty liars!" I heard the colonel burst out. Then the message was taken in and I was beckoned away.

Round I went again and down the hill. The major was shouting once more.

"Aiming point, straight edge of Gaba Tepe! Two degrees four-five minutes elevation! Corrector one-four-five-three-four hundred! One round, battery FIRE!"

The guns roared out and long flames stabbed the air.

132

A call came: "One gun out of action, sir."

"What's wrong?"

"Finding out!"

"Shorten corrector six! Drop one-fifty! FIRE!"

Having no watch, I had kept no account of time, but noticed that the morning was growing old. The sun had moved well across to our right and the last patches of shade were disappearing. I blew into the hot air and wiped a hand across my forehead.

Still the cannonade went on, still the earth trembled, still the voice behind called out new orders falling on my dazed ears. "Last target was F — next target will be registered as H!"

Then I noticed an aeroplane coming up from the south over the Turkish lines. Puffs of shrapnel followed its course. A second one sailed far to the left, a dot in the hazy distance. The man in the balloon still watched, well out of reach of the longest gun. Presently the aeroplanes faded from sight and I went back to my old pastime of staring at the beach.

Heat and howitzers, shrapnel and sunstroke, nothing could affect the buzzing throng. From my perch I looked down onto another world. Directly below lay the Red Cross jetty from where pinnaces towed long strings of boats to the hospital ships. A white flag with a red cross waved at the end of the jetty. The wounded men were carried along the planking and placed in rows on the decks of boats that lay alongside the jetty. Unhappily, the spot was raked by enemy fire and many men who had survived long periods of suffering were killed while the boats filled up.

The wharf was in the charge of a naval party, with the short-tempered old brute in blue jacket and white trousers in command. He stood in the middle of the thoroughfare, indifferent to everything, and bellowed through a megaphone to the Red Cross men. I thought that if anything happened to him there, Old Nick would have a rough time down below. Whenever the firing lulled, I heard his voice through the megaphone.

"Am taking severe stretcher cases only. Forward severe stretcher cases — I said stretcher cases only. My God, sir, are you the fool or am I?" He added something extremely rude I won't put down. As fast as the pinnaces and their loads steamed out to sea, new boats put into harbour.

Throughout that day the procession of stretchers moving to the wharf did not stop. As the boats filled with recumbent men, those who still could stand or sit erect took up any remaining space. They clambered painfully aboard with bandages round head or arm. Most of them were weary and broken, yet more than once that day a voice piped out, "Are we down-hearted?" and a chorus answered, "No!"

With shrapnel flecking the waters and too often bursting overhead, string after string of loaded boats made for the hospital ship, and with their departure the bellow came up again, "Taking severe stretcher cases only! Forward me some stretcher cases!"

The battle was wearing on. I wondered how we did on the right and if the New Zealanders had held firmly to the left.

134

Eaves beckoned, as a message had arrived from Divisional Artillery.

I went across and watched him put it laboriously to paper. "Guns in action, three o'clock five degrees east of Battleship Hill. Engage them."

I jerked the form out of Eaves's hand and started out again to take the message to the observing station.

There was exhilaration as well as danger in the scramble through the open space, where Death roamed overhead. I reached the big dugout, leaned over, tossed in the message and was given an abrupt signal to return. Down I went, slipping and springing from tuft to tuft and falling on my back somewhere near the ledge.

Just here a brainwave came along that made me aware of a four days' growth of beard. I rose up and bolted to my own funk-hole at the bottom of the line. I retrieved my shaving tackle and returned to the ledge before you could count fifty. There I lay and perspired while the voice of Major Felix called out the new target.

"Guns in action! Aiming point right-hand edge of Battleship Hill! Line of fire five degrees five minutes right! Corrector one-five-oh-three-three hundred! Angle of sight three degrees three-five minutes elevation! One round, battery FIRE!"

I fell to watching the bay again. The transports lay at anchor beyond the range of enemy guns and the battleships riding at their stations never ceased to send loud voices over the deep. Nearer to shore a thousand craft kept speeding back and forth. Now and again a monster shell rumbled out of the hills and rent a chasm in the even sea. But still the craft came and went, without turning their course a hair's breadth. Truly, luck followed us that day.

While I watched, a hideous burst of smoke and coal dust leaped from a mine-sweeper. Smoke and dust drifted away and I scanned her keenly, but could discern no damage.

Just then I saw the *Queen Elizabeth* swing around to pick up a target. She aimed at a howitzer in action on a far crest. But the shells and shrapnel burst in vain upon the howitzer's stout overhead cover. While crouching behind its sandbag ramparts it kept booming in defiance at the infidel guns.

However, the howitzer had still to meet the battleship in earnest. The good old *Queen Bess* moved further out to sea and there she lay. With cunning she laid her heavy guns and watched. Then the ship quivered and with a bellow of rage she hurled a two thousand-pound shell across the waters. It struck just below the crest of the hill. Away went the crest and away went the howitzer.

Somewhere else, drawn by ten horses, an enemy field gun trotted into the open. There the gun unlimbered and the team turned for cover. In the bay a British boat was watching, and from it leaped two flames . . . and there was a whirlwind where that Turkish gun had been. The whirlwind climbed towards the sky. There was no gun, there were no horses, there were no men.

The *Queen Bess* emptied round after round from her fifteen-inch guns, whose shrapnel spread a mile and wiped from this earth two entire companies of Turkish

136

infantry. "Allah! Oh, Allah! Thy courtyards will be filled this night!"

I was hot, tired, thirsty and sticky with perspiration. A fur had grown over the roof of my mouth, for I was unwashed and my clothes had not been taken off for almost a week. And I thought, "Damn this. Is this how life is to be for the next two years, with maybe a bullet as a final bonus?"

I looked down on the highway of the beach, where lines of wounded moved towards the boats. Under the cliffs doctors probed red wounds and carved at arms and legs. Indians urged mules, sailors toiled at guns and wagons and midget midshipmen or naval cadets ran round with revolvers strapped at their hips. A wireless man sent out his buzz-buzz, and cursing Army Service men hauled in new barges of provisions. Greeks screamed at donkeys and kept a wide eye on shelter, and sappers wielded picks. Officers of many ranks dodged from point to point and waved hands and flourished canes. Men pumped water into tanks from barges.

Then I looked out at sea, where the battleships spewed out flames and destroyers sped up and down. Men toiled at oars in boats that emptied reinforcements onto the shore. Pinnaces hooted, and loaded barges swung at their anchor. I looked and thought: "Gunner Lake, this is not the time for complaints."

I began to consider shaving myself. Every trace of shade had gone and I sat leaning forward on a bare ledge with the sun blazing in my face. "So be it," I muttered and swore while spreading out my shaving

TO HELL AND BACK

tackle. Into a pannikin went a few drops of water, sacrificing a precious drink. I picked up the soap from the sand and rubbed it over my face.

Then Eaves interrupted by waving a message form in my face. I took it without a word and started up to the observing station. My face was crusted with soap by the time I returned. Back safely in the dugout I made a second attempt at shaving, utilising a few more drops of my scarce water supply. As the ground shivered continually under the cannonade, I pictured my hand slipping and Gunner Lake going to his doom. It cost me many an oath, and several nicks on my cheek and the point of my chin, but at last victory was mine.

My eye fell on a trawler that had been fatally shelled and was going down by the stern. The water was lapping her gunwales and creeping onto the deck. While the boat sank very slowly, bursting shrapnel raked her from bow to stern at intervals. I saw the crew put off in an open boat and pull with the heart of a Yarra eight through the sea knocked up with bullets. With thundering blows the guns continued hitting the sinking boat until she disappeared below the waves. It was a violent end for the ancient fishing tub.

Up I scrambled with yet another message. When I arrived, Major Felix was shouting to his section commander: "We can't clear the crest at two-four hundred!"

Streams of wounded men on stretchers still passed below. Others staggered along the road from the head of Monash Valley, dragging themselves along in pain.

138

One Red Cross fellow with a donkey passed twice or thrice that day.

"The man with the donkey", as we called him, was becoming known to all; firing seemed not to worry him. On his donkey he would mount a man wounded in leg or foot and bring them down Monash or Shrapnel Valley to the dressing station on the beach. "The man with the donkey" was always cheerful and seemed never to tire.[28]

Now and again a mule battery, laden with guns and ammunition, wound up the narrow path like a serpent. I watched it twisting up and up the ridge until the crest came in between. At times a dead mule would stay to mark the passage.

Eaves was beckoning again. I leaned forward and caught the message. Up through the tufted grasses I went and then down again to my ledge. A few moments later I was climbing the hill once more.

"All guns ten minutes more right! Shorten corrector four. Drop five-oh. Battery FIRE!"

I was very weary of the uproar and I looked over to the Red Cross jetty. A group of sailors waited on the jetty while a string of boats drew in. I saw the puff of a shell. The sailors scattered — one poor fellow went down and another one staggered away into cover. A couple of comrades ran back, picked up the fallen man and rushed for shelter under the cliff. I could not follow what happened to them.

"Stop!" Major Felix was shouting. "Stop!" There was the roar of the firing gun. "Who fired then?" There were quick answers and quick replies. The major burst out: "Take that sergeant off that gun and put him under arrest!" There were more answers and muffled replies. "All right," the major shouted again. "Let him carry on — I'll see him after!" Again his voice roared: "Guns in action at C. Aiming point left edge of the false ridge. Line of fire five degrees on and five minutes right! Corrector one-five-oh, three-nine hundred! Angle of sight three degrees one-oh minutes elevation. One round, battery FIRE!"

Messages came hurrying through and I became exhausted with climbing up and down delivering them. Finally there was some time to sit still. I saw an infantry fellow perched on my ledge, looking hot and fagged.

I crouched beside him and asked, "How are things going? Have you heard anything?"

"Bonzer. We've got 'em on the move. They say the British are joining us at five o'clock tonight. We've been cut up a good bit, but the navy has sent thousands of the Turks sky high. We'll win all right. I was sent here with a wounded man and must get back. So long, mate."

"So long," I answered.

He watched for the sky to clear of shrapnel, pulled the rifle onto his shoulder and ambled off. "A cheerful, misinformed liar," I thought, "but a good man."

For the time my work appeared over. I was not hungry — hunger had departed long since. Divisional Artillery took a rest, so for a while I could forget the battle that raged around me. I rested against the naked brown earth until the sun laid weights on my eyelids.

The last image I saw was that of dead men and a pile of dead mules lying along the sea shore.

My eyelids became too heavy and I had to close my eyes in the end. All I could hear now was the faint sound of firing, and during the lulls the voice through the megaphone. Then my senses became oblivious to rifle fire and machine guns and all grew quiet and peaceful.

When I opened my eyes again the heat of the day had passed. The sun was much lower and fewer ships were in action.

Then I saw Eaves staring down at me and pelting me with clods of earth.

"Wake up, mate," he yelled. "Get up and take this message!"

Suddenly I was fully awake and sat up straight. I stood up and blinked, took the form and started on another climb. On the way I ran into Sergeant-major Gardiner and Wilkinson, who were coming down.

Gardiner held up a bullet in his fingers. "Lake, look at this — you nearly needed a new sergeant-major. My belt stopped this one."

CHAPTER
EIGHT

IN THE ANZAC TRENCHES

A couple of mornings later the telephonist on duty pulled me from my sleep. As usual I cursed him, and as usual I bowed to circumstances and sat up.

It was still pitch dark and the air was clear and sharp. It was fairly quiet if one forgot the roll of rifle fire, but no shells passed over to the sea. Standing in the dark I pulled on my clothes and lastly picked up the overcoat, which I had used as a blanket. I fastened my coat collar round my ears and pulled my woollen cap down low to meet the collar. Over one shoulder went the bandolier. With my tucker bag around my waist I was ready.

I looked at the bay with a multitude of craft on its bosom — lights were winking and winking forever. The sky was like a giant's blue punch bowl, picked out from rim to centre with points of golden light.

Two figures moved near the observing station and I climbed up to them. They were Cliffe and Wilkinson, who was loaded up with telephones and a white tucker bag. Wilkinson, whose head was hidden in a muffler, gave me a nod. Both men must have been waiting for me, for Cliffe whispered, "Are you ready, Lake?"

We set off at once and had to pick a careful way through dugouts where sleepers, rolled from head to foot in blankets, blocked the road. The advance over the broken hillside became easier when we picked up a shepherd's track, which led us up the valley. Once on that path we went forward at a steady pace — dawn was due in half an hour, and by then we must have reached the trenches. The valley held snipers, and after daybreak we would be exposed to enemy shrapnel from head to foot. It was no place for mass meetings.

It was deucedly cold! I stuffed my hands into my pockets and the others did the same. We marched in Indian file, for the path itself was narrow and full of ups and downs, and seemingly ever rising. We went always at the same hard pace and said very little, unless the direction became uncertain.

In the open I had become used to the dark, but down here in the valley it was impossible to make out anything further away than a yard or two. On both sides steep and rugged land went up, covered with low, scrubby bushes, enough to hide an army of snipers.

The path wound about and about and was much broken in places. Probably it had been raining lately or mountain streams crept down this way, as at times we were splashing through heavy mud and puddles. We had to jump from tussock to tussock to keep our shoes dry. As we got higher matters became a bit better, and next we were losing ourselves among the hills.

Cliffe guided the way and I was the last of the three. I saw Cliffe's small figure dimly four or five yards ahead, moving this way and that among the bushes, sometimes putting a hand out to push branches aside. Then followed Wilkinson, taller, narrower, and loaded up like a packhorse. Neither ever turned a head. Where the path broadened to a road we saw several dead mules.

Three or four hundred yards beyond we suddenly heard whispering voices. Next moment we were into the tail of at least a score of men. They formed an uncertain line along the track and were in full marching order, with their packs up. They were either coming from or going to the firing line. Then I recognised them as a party of Marines, who had arrived the previous night to reinforce us. They filled the path, obliging us to slow down. From the hurried whispers, I gathered that they had lost their way; a sergeant was bustling up and down in an attempt to keep them together. They stared at us curiously.

As our way was blocked we stepped off the path and pushed through the bushes for a little distance until we were ahead of them. Somebody in front, who appeared to be in charge, started a muffled conversation with Cliffe. "You'd better hurry," advised Cliffe. "By daybreak the place is dosed with shrapnel."

After this encounter the going became much harder. Although there was still a path, we had to climb rather than walk. After a few minutes I became so warm I could easily have left my coat behind.

All the time we passed Marines in small groups of three and four. Though now much broken up, they must all have belonged to one large party moving to the trenches. In spite of the steep incline we travelled quickly, as dawn was already near.

Eventually we arrived at a spot high up on the hill, where the path turned abruptly to the left. I was glad to halt there for a few moments and sat down on the bank, throwing open my coat collar. I became aware that the faint greyness of dawn had crept over the world. On either side were vague contours of bushes, and the country revealed itself full of shallow trenches and funk-holes, which yawned like endless graves. I grew aware of many men sleeping in those shelters. There were tins of beef and bags of biscuit near them and the ashes of yesterday's fires. I wondered what the men were doing here, so far behind the firing line.

Cliffe sat cross-legged on a tussock, his chin in his hands. All of a sudden he looked round and began to speak. "Look at these fellows," he said. "I can't make out how it is allowed to go on. Every man there ought to be in the firing line. Instead of that they skulk about here all day with plenty of tucker. I'm pretty sure most of them haven't even seen the trenches yet."

"Why is nothing being done?" I asked.

Cliffe replied, "I believe they're starting to do something, but things have been in a muddle. The battalions are mixed up and no one knows who is dead and who still alive — that's the excuse, I suppose. Last night I was coming up here after poor Byers was shot. I spoke to one lot with a fire going, who were filling themselves with bully beef and jam. When I asked them what they were doing, one fellow gave me cheek, so I pulled out my revolver. It made him change his attitude."

Cliffe continued: "Later on I met an officer who had lost his way, his men and everything else. He came to me and asked if I could direct him — he was nearly incoherent. There was some shrapnel about at the time and as each shell burst he dived under cover and refused to come out. I spoke to him roughly in the end, though he was senior to me, and finally he started to cry. I left him there."[29]

After Cliffe had stopped his monologue, Wilkinson, who sat crouched on the bank, began to speak in his rapid way, voicing his disgust at cowardice.

"We'd better make another start," Cliffe said. "It isn't far."

Even now there was no trace of dawn in the sky, but the greyness I had noticed was more marked and I could make out the leaves on the bushes. It was quite possible to see the way underfoot and to avoid the numerous trenches zig-zagging about here. We struck the firm path again a little further on and from that point the road climbed quickly. We had marched perhaps five minutes, and objects were growing clearer.

Something moved through the sky, then there was a bang, followed by a pattering and rustling in the bushes some way behind us. Overhead floated a delicate puff of smoke. The concert had opened.

"There goes the first!" Wilkinson cried.

"Aye," I said and Cliffe nodded his head.

We had little breath for remarks and went on as quickly as we could. The half light had penetrated everywhere, although still there were no signs in the sky. But the shrapnel had clapped over our heads and we knew what would follow. When we turned to the left we stumbled on a fresh grave marked by pebbles and a rough cross. We took half a turn to the right and then I found myself entering a tunnel with no top. The walls sloped down as we went on, until they were no more than four feet high.

"Duck," said Cliffe and set the example. Moving at half a run we ducked for several yards. Then the walls rose higher up again and soon we could stand upright. I looked about and found we were in the trenches.

As it was now completely light, we could make out everything. This trench seemed seven, perhaps eight foot deep, and must have been a spot of special importance, as it was well widened out. Further on it narrowed again to the width of the passage by which we entered and took a sharp turn; we could see no further.

The trench was full of men in dull green uniforms, who sat and lay in scooped-out recesses, or stood and blocked the narrow passage. Their rifles rested along the trench walls, some with bayonets fixed, some without. For a long time I had not seen so many Englishmen together. Their faces struck me as kind. They looked at us with interest when we came in and marched across to the corner reserved for artillery observation. A lieutenant with a brown woollen cap on his head leaned from a funk-hole, perched somewhat higher than the others. He started to ask us questions, but no one else spoke.

"Who are you?" the lieutenant asked, leaning round.

"We've come here to observe for the artillery. This is the place we've always used," Cliffe answered without turning his head. "You must have relieved our fellows in the night."

"Oh, you're *Australians*! Yes, we arrived last night." No more was said.

We settled ourselves. Wilkinson connected one of the telephones and attached himself to it; he gave a second one to a knock-kneed person who appeared from nowhere. Cliffe began to prepare his lookout a couple of yards away. I found myself a comfortable place to sit; there was no work for me unless the wire along the valley was cut by shrapnel or spies. A third telephonist joined us, lying on his back in a funk-hole beside me.

The trenches were topped with a rampart made of sandbags, which had been dumped on top of each other in a double row. The observer had the risky task of having to peer through a small hole between the sandbags. While sitting, the rampart was no more than a foot above our heads. Cliffe and I started to pull the sandbags aside, leaving several gaps through which the whole landscape could be viewed. I looked through one of the gaps and saw a stretch of desolate country, sloping up towards some hills. In the grey light I saw that it was covered with patches of heath and low bushes. Here and there wildflowers were springing up. Enemy trenches were easy to spot by their sandbagged parapets and mounds of newly turned earth. They ran parallel with ours, and were only a short distance away.

Not one living Turk could be seen. But their presence was unmistakable, as in many places the swift

148

movement of a shovel appeared above the parapet. Like us, the Turks were digging for their lives.

Now that our climb was over, I felt cold again, so I kept my coat on. Cliffe and Wilkinson were hardier, and after a good deal of turning around and thumping and scratching, they made their coats into some sort of armchairs in an attempt to defeat the uncharitable hard ground. I settled back in a funk-hole and took stock of recent events. The rifle fire on both sides was brisk, loud and continuous. Frequently a machine gun rattled away for a few minutes, ending as abruptly as it began. Near the trench entrance, where the parapet was lowest, bullets plumped over into the opposite bank and sent up tiny fountains of dust. By now many shrapnel shells were coming over as well, but the valley was their target, and they searched it with care from top to bottom.

On the opposite bank, not far from me, was the grave of one of our men. An upright bayonet had been pushed into the ground and from it hung a soldier's belt. Below was placed a soldier's hat. There were no words of farewell or stones to mark a square of earth, but at intervals an odd bullet splashed down there and beat a tattoo. "My friend," I thought, "I vouch there are only few bitterer graves than yours."

It was a chilly business sitting there while the sun climbed above the horizon. In the end the sun came over a hill, but the trench walls cut away its beams. The men sat very still; they talked in low tones or were dozing. For the present the telephonists were unoccupied, and lay on their sides in a bored manner.

149

Every now and then Cliffe took a peep through one of his holes, but there were too many stray bullets to make the occupation healthy.

To pass the time I decided on a breakfast of jam and biscuits, to be washed down with a draught of stale water. Without troubling to get up I unhitched my tucker bag and found a tin of bully beef, a tin of plum jam and a lot of the hard biscuits we had been given before landing. I left the beef for later and dipped the biscuits into the jam, taking care to bring out more jam than biscuit.

I could hear the Englishmen talking among themselves. They spoke with a broad accent and I gathered they were from up north.

"It's a bitterly cold place here, chum," I heard one say.

"You won't be saying that in a few hours' time," I replied. "It'll be as hot as blazes here."

Everybody looked at me and one or two grinned, but nobody spoke. They seemed to regard Australians as interesting, and admired them. Apparently our name as fighters was made when we took the place.[30] I fixed on the nearest fellow.

"What part of the old country d'you come from, pal?"

"Manchester," he replied and that was all he said. No one else had the wish to talk, so before long I went back to my hard biscuits and jam.

Time went on, and as it drew towards seven o'clock the men brightened up and moved about more and cracked a few jokes. I was still as cold as charity and kept looking for the sun to climb up and send a little warmth over the parapet. Since our appearance on the scene, a man or two had been working with pick and shovel, deepening the trench. In desperation to get warm I finally got up from my funk-hole and took a hand at the work myself, until getting out of breath.

I had just given the tools back when the words "the colonel" were passed from mouth to mouth. A party of officers came into the trench on a tour of inspection. The British colonel who led the way was a middle-aged man wearing a woollen cap. He did not look like a soldier; he looked more like a businessman who had never attempted anything more exciting than catching a tram after breakfast.

"Why isn't this trench deeper?" he wanted to know. "That's not the way to shovel, man — give me the spade. There, that's the way to do it. Now start, men, start! Don't stand there idling."

The lieutenant was leaning out of his funk-hole with an anxious face. The colonel looked up at him without much kindness. "A Company is somewhere along here, isn't it?" he demanded.

"Yes, sir. Straight along. You must keep down; these trenches are very shallow."

"I'm going there now. Keep these men digging. Don't let them slacken off!" And on the colonel went, bending down and scrambling out at the further end, his retinue following in silence.

No doubt there were quite a few amateurs here. On our right they had unwisely rigged a machine gun among the bushes on top of the parapet. The situation was murder — for us, not the enemy. There was no cover, and firing the gun meant crouching among the bushes, providing an easy target for Turkish bullets.

A sergeant was in charge of the gun and lay on his stomach up there observing the enemy's movements and sending down reports every few minutes. For some reason the lieutenant in charge made no effort to keep the gun secret, but at frequent intervals ordered fifteen or twenty rounds of rapid fire, so that our corner attracted growing interest from the enemy. A conversation ensued.

"Still there, sergeant?"

"Yes, sir."

"Anything to be seen?"

"No, sir. Nothing important — digging going on in one place. A lot of dirt goes up."

"Well, give 'em a burst there; it'll keep their heads down. A short burst — not more than twenty."

Silence followed, then bang-bang, bang-bang went the gun.

"Any results, sergeant?"

"Not sure, sir — I think they've stopped digging."

A few minutes later the lieutenant enquired: "Anything to be seen, sergeant?"

"Nothing special, sir. I saw a man look over the parapet just now."

"Well, give him a burst. Five or six will do — jolly them up a little."

Bang-bang, bang-bang, bang-bang went the gun again.

Cliffe proved something of a sportsman. He borrowed my rifle and sniped away at intervals through his peephole. I don't know what he saw to shoot at any more than I could discover where all the rifle fire came from.

All of a sudden Cliffe called out to me in an excited whisper, "D'you want a shot, Lake? There's an old Turk here poking his head up."

I jumped up and took hold of the rifle. Cliffe was staring through one of the holes. "Look through here after me," he said. "He's right ahead, about six hundred yards off."

I took a long look, but could not pick him up.

"Do you see the dead fellow in blue trousers?"

I saw the dead Turk all right, lying spread out in a patch of flowers; then, thirty yards or more to the right, I saw something move. Sure enough, it was a man.

"Got him," I said, lifting my head over the parapet to level the rifle . . . but I had been too long, and friend Turk disappeared. I stayed ready for some time in case he came back, but he never showed up again. Instead the cold morning breeze drifted against my forehead and climbed into my hair. I had a strange feeling looking across that wasteland and watching our bullets strike the opposite trenches, being aware that at any moment Death might arrive in the form of a Turkish bullet.

"Don't keep your head up too long, Lake," Cliffe said presently. "It isn't over-healthy." I took his advice.

Time went very slowly. I tried to talk to Wilkinson and then to Cliffe, but there was nothing to talk about.

153

The Englishmen became more and more depressed, and finally nobody spoke at all except for the lieutenant, who never seemed to lose interest in his gun. Now and then he also called out directions to the men who were shovelling in the passageway.

The rifle fire continued all the while, and many a bullet knocked up the dust on the opposite bank three or four yards off. From the hour of our landing the fire had not ceased for a moment, but up here the noise was sharper, fiercer and closer at hand than down on the beach.

Enemy shrapnel passed constantly over our heads, though I don't think it did much harm, for it fell in the valley, which was generally empty, except for a few skulkers who knew how to look after themselves.

Our own guns remained silent. I sat and shivered and felt bored beyond belief. At last matters improved.

"You're wanted on the phone, sir," Wilkinson said.

"Who wants me?" asked Cliffe.

"The colonel, sir."

Cliffe crept the two or three paces to the phone and put it to his mouth. "Hullo! Hullo there! Yes, Cliffe speaking." A long pause.

"Yes, I've got it. C target. Three o'clock right of false ridge. Straight away. Right-ho, sir."

Back went Cliffe to his peepholes to stare through one of them. "They seem to have woken up down below at last," he said. "The old balloon has spotted some guns in action three o'clock right of the false ridge up there. There's one of them now!" We waited a minute or two, crouching down below the parapet, then

Wilkinson, who had the phone strapped to his head, said, "Fired, sir."

The voice of a gun travelled from the valley foot, and at the same moment a shell swept over our heads and burst in a puff of smoke hundreds of yards beyond us. I was staring through one of the peepholes. The shot was over the target and rather to the left.

"One degree three-oh minutes more right! Shorten corrector four! Drop two-oh-oh! Repeat!" Wilkinson echoed the words. A silence followed, then the gun boomed below and another shell whistled overhead. This time the burst was better. "Drop five-oh! Repeat!" Cliffe called out.

Presently I moved away and tried again to talk with the Englishmen. Nearly all were young and none seemed over-bright. By the time we had exchanged all news, the morning was wearing on. Finally the sun tossed his beams into the trench in a threatening manner.

These were still optimistic days, when we expected British and French soldiers down south to join up with us at any moment. We always believed, hearing their guns and daily reports coming through, that they were arriving at such and such an hour. Today it was to be five o'clock in the afternoon.

The village of Krithia had been taken, and Heaven knows what else besides. At any instant now the British and French ought to come pouring over the top of Achi Baba. The optimists among us believed the fall of Constantinople was only a matter of days. The Marines were as confident as we Australians and the expectation that the whole affair would be over within a week or two was the one thing that kept them going. But they were a homesick lot.

Our guns soon quietened down — no doubt shortage of ammunition — and Cliffe left his post and came across where the trench was deeper, to stretch his legs. The English lieutenant was sitting just above and the two men drifted into conversation.

I had the luck to find a magazine with a sentimental love story inside. I carried it to my funk-hole, made a comfortable bed and read until the springs of romance welled in me. I fell asleep to dream of governesses, dukes and heiresses who smiled encouragement on poor broken-down gunners. When I woke up it must have been midday, as the sun was not far from the centre of the sky and there was not a foot of shade.

I looked around and found that nothing had changed. The men sat in the same places and talked with effort. Cliffe spoke to Wilkinson and the sergeant lay beside his gun. I yawned and sat up, flapped at the flies and swore.

Throughout the endless afternoon nothing changed. At times our guns opened fire and Cliffe observed for them. At times I peeped over the parapet, hoping to snipe a Turk, and at times the machine gun rattled away. There was little movement on either side. The armies rested after the big attack. I don't know who was best pleased when the light grew dim and orders came through to return to headquarters.

★　★　★

The following afternoon I met the Marines once again. I had guided Major Felix to the trench and there we found Sands observing, with Hawkins and Eaves as his telephonists.

The same Marines were in the same places and digging was going forward as before. The trench had been improved during the night and was deeper and more secure. But on the other hand I noticed the rifle fire was very heavy and enemy shells were bursting unpleasantly close. Major Felix and I had one or two uneasy moments coming up the valley, so it was disappointing to find we were not to be left alone here.

Eaves sprawled on his back with the receiver strapped to his ear.

"Hullo," he called out genially when he saw me. "What are you doin' 'ere?" I nodded to him and climbed nearer to Hawkins, who sat higher up than Eaves under the lee of the bank.

"How's things?" I asked, settling down.

"It's been pretty hot all day," he answered, putting down the transmitter and taking out a cigarette. "This morning they lobbed two or three percussion shells onto the wall over there. They're after the machine gun. Those fools: they'll never leave the thing alone for five minutes."

Eaves tried to get a match from someone and eventually succeeded. Then he went on. "That gun ought to be taken out of the place — otherwise they'll have us blown out of this hole in the end."

We yarned away a long time. I don't know what happened to Major Felix; he had disappeared. I stayed

157

on, having no orders to return. The longer I stayed, the hotter grew the rifle fire. Our own guns in the valley were active and kept Sands fully occupied peering through his peepholes and giving contradictory orders to the telephonists. The Turkish guns were more aggressive than our own. Frequent shells came our way, bursting about fifty yards behind us and dismembering the bushes.

Presently, while enjoying a rare moment of silence, word came down the line that the enemy was massing on our right. This woke the trench up. Two officers of the Marines were present at the time. One — the lieutenant we had met the day before — sat in his funk-hole (his favourite spot), commanding this corner of the trench; the other officer had been giving instructions about the digging. They exchanged excited glances. "Where did the message come from? Who passed the message down?" they demanded in one voice. Someone answered, "The message came by mouth down the trench, sir."

"Is that the whole message? Was there anything more? Is anything to be seen?"

"I don't know, sir."

The officer in the funk-hole leaned out and looked up towards the machine gun. "Are you there, sergeant?"

"No, sir," was the answer. "I'm here."

"Well, can you see anything? Can you see any special movement?"

There was no reply for a while. Then I heard, "No, sir, I can't see anything in particular."

Sands was called into consultation. His verdict, given in disinterested voice, bore out what the sergeant had said. But all the while the fire from both sides was increasing. Bullets plumped time after time into our opposite bank and a multitude of shells travelled forwards and backwards across the sky. I began to feel warlike. Rapid conversations went on between the officers, but as nothing further happened, the excitement died a natural death. We were settling comfortably into our places again when a second message came along. "Enemy massing heavily on our right. Attack expected."

This settled matters. The place buzzed like a beehive. Sands was appealed to again. "Can you see no movements at all from where you are?"

"Absolutely nothing," Sands answered, in the blandest manner, and without turning round. A moment afterwards he called to me over his shoulder, "Climb up by the machine gun, Lake, and try to observe the next two shots. I can't pick them up from here. I should try not to get killed if I were you. You probably will be, anyhow."

I did as he told me and lay flat on my stomach beside the machine gun. There was absolutely no cover, so I flattened out to the last inch and looked across the same wilderness as yesterday. Our bullets knocked up the dust along the Turkish line and our shells broke in delicate white clouds about the sky. I could not see a single living Turk. I had not much opportunity to look about, as I had to closely watch the ground on which one of our guns was trained. I saw the puff at last and

159

called out the direction. Sands answered that he too had picked it up.

While I was flat out calculating how soon a bullet would come my way, a very young lieutenant walked over. "I say, keep down as much as you can," he warned, lifting up his face to me, "or you will draw fire on us."

"You bloody fool, what do you think I am doing?" I thought.

"Yes, sir," was all I said.

At four o'clock the men in the trench were due to be relieved by another company; despite the critical situation, they made themselves ready to depart. Quite soon the relieving company found their way in. They carried fixed bayonets and looked like business. The trench was choked up, and being in the way, I climbed into a nearby funk-hole.

I was lucky to have left the trench. Officers of the old party were hunting their men out, causing general confusion. Suddenly there was a loud explosion nearby; stones and clouds of dust shot up, followed by silence. A percussion shell had come into the trench. The senior officer beside me craned his neck forward and called out, in a voice sharp with anxiety, to know whether anyone was hurt.

"Forbes killed, sir, and two others hit bad."

"Get them away to the doctor at once — don't block up the way!"

The soldiers pushed themselves against the walls and the procession of wounded went by. The dead man came last. I peered from my funk-hole and looked him in the face. I did not think he was quite dead, but I heard someone say in a stage whisper that his back was broken. His face was yellow and his mouth a little open — death had not stamped him with nobility.

The new company squeezed against the trench sides and the old one filed away. The firing from both sides was overwhelming and our trench bristled with bayonets. I had seen nothing threatening in the movements of the enemy when I was up by the gun, but excitement ran high and I caught it. Matters began to look really interesting when a call came for reinforcements on the right.

Amid inquiries and commands, a sergeant was sent off at express speed with a party to find out details; at the same time the trench began to fill up again with the men who had been relieved. Next an officer pushed his way along, revolver in hand. Indecision seemed so great that I began to doubt whether we could hold the trench in the event of a rush. I made myself ready for the worst, fixed a bayonet to my rifle and prepared to die as becomes an honest gunner.

Within five minutes the sergeant came back.

"They want no reinforcements, sir. There's nothing out of the way doing. They made a demonstration on the right, sir, and attacked our left."

On the way back to headquarters, we found the top of the valley lined with men lying on their bellies, rifles in hand and bayonets fixed.

The next day another tragedy occurred in that corner of the trench. The Marines had been relieved by an

Australian battalion. I was on duty in the trench in the afternoon and was about to leave when a shell came in. I swung round towards the uproar and at that moment something struck me on the foot. I looked down and saw a lump of quivering flesh. The neck of a captain of infantry had been blown away.

I returned down the valley, sick to death. Shrapnel was spattering in the bushes, and at the crossroads lay three dead mules, blood still flowing from their carcasses. I hurried along, but could not escape the horrifying image of the captain's mangled head. I could not eat that night, and though thirsty, I threw away my tea. I rolled into my blankets, but still that lump of flesh floated in front of my eyes. Darkness and the cool of night had no power to banish such a vision.

CHAPTER
NINE

BEAUTY AMONG THE CARNAGE

Shortly afterwards Lieutenant Sands singled me out as his victim to attend him on a telephone-laying expedition. I felt unwilling to receive this honour, which involved getting up at half-past three in the morning.

On the way from the dugout I met Sands wandering round the cookhouse like an uneasy ghost. He ignored my existence for several minutes but shot a glance at me more than once out of the corner of his eye, though he spoke no word and went on with whatever he was doing.

At last he pushed his hands into his pockets and started off into the dark. "Come along, Lake, and take that reel with you," he said over his shoulder.

I picked up the hand reel with telephone wire and hurried after him. We followed a track along the dugouts and went down into the valley. Clear starlight was overhead, but it was absolutely dark down there. I had no idea where we were going, or how far, but soon discovered we were moving towards our right wing.

We took the communication trench which ran from our observing station, followed it to the end and reached the edge of the big valley. But instead of turning up the valley Sands went straight across. We passed an Indian Army camp on our left. There was nothing to betray its existence until we heard the stamping of mules. Then we picked up a small path winding round the bottom of the hill. I remembered passing that way a day or two before. Sands continued to push on a pace or two ahead of me. Presently, without turning his head or making any movement, he called back: "Do you know where A Battery is, Lake?"

"Yes, sir, I was there two days ago."

"It's moved since then."

"Then I have no idea where it is."

"Neither have I," he said with a laugh.

"Are we supposed to go to A Battery?" I asked.

"Of course. We have to lay a wire from headquarters to the battery's observing station."

"Then why haven't we brought a guide, sir?"

"What do we want a guide for? I was halfway there myself yesterday. I have a good general idea where the place is, and I was given details last night. Come on, Lake, we mustn't waste time — this isn't a good place to be after daybreak."

At those words I began to doubt whether that young lieutenant knew what he was doing.

The walk soon worked away my drowsiness. I wished we had been on a more peaceful errand, for this part of the coast was magnificent. It was warmer than I had yet known at such an early hour. In fact, I found it too warm for scrambling up those steep hills.

A multitude of stars looked down on us with an unfathomable gaze. The little winds that met us ran in and out of the bushes, flip-flapping the smaller leaves and stirring the larger ones. The scents of spring flowers floated down with a strength and sweetness that the day never let them keep. The heavy dew on the bushes splashed my forehead and my hands with cool drops. I caught some leaves, rubbed my hands in them and so had my first wash for the day.

In that silent, starry night we pushed on to prepare for fresh destruction. I could not hear a sound or catch a movement of beast or bird, but feared that Turkish eyes might be looking out from the bushes.

The gunfire rolled on, and lights were winking in the bay, attesting that men were everywhere on land and at sea.

We came to a steep narrow gully, which turned at right angles from the path. "This is the shortest way to the old position of A Battery, sir," I said.

"Lead the way, Lake," Sands commanded.

"But you said they had moved, sir."

"Go on, Lake, lead the way — it will bring us somewhere near them. One way is as good as another."

Sands clearly had no idea where the battery was! Good God!

I led the way. The path was easy for a hundred yards but then it became necessary to clamber up some difficult cliffs. Eventually I came to a full stop and turned round.

"This is the way to the old location," I said and pointed up.

165

Sands eyed it pensively. "Is that the only way?"

"There is a longer but much easier road, which sweeps round the hill. Shall we take that?"

"Yes. Hurry up, Lake. It's late already — the sun will soon be up. We'll be dead men if we waste time here." The lieutenant's words sounded alarming, but he did not seem worried at the prospect.

Complete darkness favoured us, but dawn would not long delay, so I agreed that it was time to hurry. In a few minutes we were back on the main path. We followed it over the shoulder of a hill. The climb was steep and soon we had to steady our pace. Wherever we went the country was covered with low bushes and destitute of a single sizeable tree. Eventually, the path turned left and climbed to the summit of the hill. I continued on along that path, which led directly to the old position of A Battery. But Sands stopped and peered down into the next valley.

"No, this is the way," he said. "I'm pretty certain the guns have been taken somewhere over there." He started along a road that dipped straight down and ran in the direction of Gaba Tepe.

There was a wide view of the ocean from here and a salty breeze drifted from the waters. Whether Sands discovered poetry in that scene or not I cannot say, but he stood still with his head to one side, eyeing the shadowy waters. The reverie lasted only a few moments. "It will soon be light, Lake," he said. "If we don't find the guns, we'll probably both be dead in half an hour."

In his voice there was neither anxiety nor interest; he made the statement as one might remark that the evening was excellent for a walk.

We said no more all the way down the slope. I became worried that he had no idea where we were, where we were going, or what was to happen to us. It was the usual mess and muddle. I was convinced that Gaba Tepe was straight ahead and saw us lost among the wire entanglements, waiting to be hit by snipers as soon as it was light enough.

A stiff hill rose directly ahead, and the world was vague and grey with the approach of dawn. Sands looked at the steep hill and once or twice threw a sideways glance at me. Finally he swore feebly and started to climb.

We followed a road which may have been made by sappers, who seemed able to make roads wherever they liked; it was wide, and seemed smooth enough. I climbed along the side of the road and helped myself onward by pulling at the bushes. By now I was full of venom towards Sands for risking both our lives with his habitual lack of preparation. For his part, he said nothing at all; he just breathed heavily, perspired, and toiled on.

Some distance up, the road became less steep and crossed another one. To my astonishment the crossroad showed fresh wheel tracks. Being unsure, Sands gaped a moment — then he said nonchalantly, "I knew it had to be about here, Lake. A Battery will be somewhere on top of the hill. But we have to hurry — dawn's coming and shrapnel will come down any minute now."

We followed the wheel tracks up the hill, but had to slow our pace. Further on we ran into a camp of sappers. The guard told us that guns had passed by during the night, so we kept following the gun tracks. After rounding a corner, we came upon an artillery camp and a field gun.

A few men were up and about, but many were still rolled up in their blankets. The guard directed us to the nearby battery and soon we entered the communication trenches. They ran this way and that, so we were constantly asking the way. It was hard to avoid the men who were asleep on the barren earth. A string of oaths followed our progress.

Finally, we arrived at the battery observing station, where we found Major Felix and several of his men. I took a seat in the background and watched how the major's face clouded over as Sands explained his errand. I could not overhear what was said.

Sands beckoned me with a jerk of his head. "We have to lay the telephone line to here," he said. "Last night Jones and I brought the drum halfway up the valley — we must find it again."

So we were only starting the operation!

The battery was on top of a large flat hill and the guns were not yet properly dug in. As we arrived, gangs of men were shovelling earth and others dragged masses of bushes along to hide the guns from aircraft observation. Everyone worked at top speed, but I could see that they would not finish by daybreak.

Sands led me over waste country, covered with stunted bushes, coarse grasses and a few flowering

168

plants. Countless exploded Turkish shells lay among the grass and in some places the turf was torn up by heavy fire.

When the lieutenant had prophesied our destruction at dawn, he must have felt that it was here we could be killed. Fortunately, this morning started quietly enough, with only the distant roll of rifle fire.

Sands seemed to have lost his bearings again. Once we passed a dead infantryman sprawled among the long grasses. The body had been overlooked, and was now decaying — the stench of the rotting corpse was tainting the morning air for dozens of yards around. The lieutenant looked long and hard at the unpleasant sight, but he made no comment.

Presently we arrived at the head of the gully. "Here we are," Sands said, coming to a halt and waving his hand. "The drum is somewhere down there." I looked down and realised what a mess he had led me into.

The country was difficult, but daylight helped us find the best tracks through the tangled undergrowth. We went on, slipping and sliding a great part of the way and scraping our shins. Suddenly we found the drum. I was ready for Sands to say he knew it had been there all the time, but he was busy catching his breath and said nothing. We rested a little while with the fresh breezes moving about us. Daylight had found a way into every recess; one or two venturesome insects were abroad already and one or two birds were singing.

Here and there — in ones, in twos, in threes — were graves of fallen soldiers, marked with improvised tokens. A couple of twigs bound together to form a

169

cross marked one, a piece of board with date and initials a second, an upright rifle a third. Already the dwarf hollies were closing around them; already the stunted laurels were bending over them.

Then began the climb back. It had been difficult before and now it was worse. We stopped at the tallest bushes to tie the wire onto them. On the way up we found an easier but longer track. Halfway up the hill the cable on the big drum ended, so for the remainder of the distance we had to use wire from the small hand reel I was carrying.

On our arrival at A Battery observing station we found it deserted. We fastened the wire to the phone and left.

While we passed the open space on the hilltop for the third time we heard a whizz and a bang, right overhead. Shrapnel came down with a whistling sound, missing us by less than a yard. Sands stopped dead, and I knew at once he was going to say something.

"You know, Lake, I'm very disappointed. I wanted to see a real battle. This is only a sniping expedition."

I said not a word.

Further on Sands stopped to adjust the position of the telephone wire. He took the wire in his hand and began bounding it into the air in an attempt to throw it over the top of a high shrub. I went to help him, but he waved me away. "You can go on, Lake, and get some breakfast. I'll follow in a minute."

I sauntered on, expecting him to overtake me very soon. At the end of the path I turned the corner and came in full view of the ocean. The stars had faded in the sky and a thousand lights of a young and pure morning fell about the ocean in cascades of silver and blue. All over the place small playful waves were bobbing — wavelets of silver and azure. On those radiant seas rode the noblest fleet that ever had sailed that way. There were ships of war: leviathans and cockleshells, all awaiting the call of morning. Scores of tiny smoke clouds climbed from the breakfast fires along the beach and at sea a hundred funnels were smoking. Up they rose in tones of blue and grey, climbing on, then fading into the morning light.

A mountain of snowy clouds was heaped along the blue horizon. So still they lay, so purely white they shone, they seemed to form a barrier to an enchanted land. While I watched, the sun rose up from that bed of virgin clouds and melted them away. On the horizon lay the isle of Imbros, clad in the splendour of the dawn. Saffron, purple, violet and many other colours of nature's magic paint box floated about the mountain peaks of the island. The contours of Imbros became clearer and clearer as a veil of mist dissolved and lost itself in the shimmering sea.

I was overcome by the sight and bowed my head as though I stood on holy ground.

Sands's crunching step amongst the rocks woke me from my reverence. I glanced round and found him level with me. At once I forgave him his foolhardiness: the expedition had brought me in sight of this unforgettable spectacle.

★ ★ ★

A number of days after our arrival I went up some of the valleys, pushing my way through the scrub. All the way I tumbled on relics of the first advance. It saddened me to look about. Boxes of ammunition had been abandoned in the undergrowth — hundreds of thousands of rounds lay spilled about for the dew to dampen and blacken them. Cases of jam, big yellow cheeses, sacks of bully beef lay there unclaimed, except by such runaways as were on the lookout for a dinner. Once I found a dead donkey, loaded up and about to start on a journey.

And the scrub held other secrets. As you peered among the shadows you might find the grizzly remains of men, lying stiller than the leaves in the hot noon. They had become horrid black and swollen figures, causing you to turn and push for more open spaces. At times a sickly wind would drift over, warning of more spots to be left alone.

It was not that we were careless with our dead and left them where they died. But some men fell in lonely places and some lay under enemy fire where the search parties could not go. In the strangest, most difficult, most wayward places little graves were dug, each with simple marks of a man's name, which winter rains would wash away.[31]

Some fenced graveyards had been made, with level rows of graves and a wooden cross at the head of each.

There were also many Turkish prizes for those who sought them. Choked rifles, a clip of cartridges, a belt or a water bottle marked the path of an earlier battle.

172

There was no end of empty shell cases and fuse caps, but I did not even bother to turn them over.

As soon as the guns fell silent, fatigue parties were sent abroad to bring in these materials. And curio hunters, and people who cannot pass an object without taking it, combed the deserted battleground for whatever had been overlooked. At one time there was regular trade with the Navy, who gave a loaf of bread for any empty Turkish shell case.

One morning I had a yarn outside our funk-hole with Thompson, Stone, Prince and one or two others. We sat in the open on biscuit tins or stones and enjoyed the mild morning sun. There was nothing to do so we talked and talked.

The endless gunfire rolled on and on from the valley's head and enemy shells burst haphazardly along the beach and over the sea. Fortunately, for an hour or more headquarters had been free from such attention, and that was all that concerned us. Old Ned Thompson had grown homesick again and was holding forth on his pet theory that after six months' active service the Government would send home all those men who wanted to go. His reasoning seemed faulty to us but he convinced himself.

Fragile clouds passed across the sun and darkened its face. The breeze rustled over the few bushes that had been spared the cook's axe. I was stirring Welsh rarebit in a mess-tin lid, watching my cooking through its critical moments.

Just then a gust of smoke filled my eyes. As my ears cleared, Thompson turned to move away, and at that instant a shell struck him with a dull sound. He breathed a long drawn-out "Oh!", threw his hands forward and fell to the ground. He managed to get up again but fell down once more.

The doctor, who had seen it happen, ran towards us. Together we carried Thompson under the shelter of the cookhouse and laid him on his back. His eyes were shut and his breathing was loud and difficult. Red Cross orderlies joined us.

The doctor leaned forward and pulled up Ned's shirt, baring his chest. Below the heart was a red wound. None of us said a word. The doctor took a syringe of morphine from his case and pushed it into the dying man's arm.

A second shell burst upon the hill and a third further along. Shells began to fall about us and burst close by. We huddled against the cookhouse and each of us wondered if he would be hit next.

Gunner Prince, who was on the other side of Thompson, seemed to have lost his head. He threw his arms out as though to push away the shells that burst around him. The dust rose thicker and thicker, turning the sun into a sullen red ball; the sea was almost hidden behind a wall of red dust.

Thompson turned his head once more — it was the last time he moved. The rasping of his breath grew feebler and feebler. The doctor sat with his back to us, his head bowed. It seemed he did not turn his eyes from the dying man. Beside him the medical orderlies

174

huddled together for cover as the shells continued to swoop down with a roar, scattering the dust. Nobody said anything as we watched the still figure of Ned Thompson and listened to his fading breath.

At last the firing passed further along the slope and the dust settled once more. The adjutant came down from his dugout. He looked at Thompson and asked, "Is it bad?"

"The bullet went in below the heart. He's still alive, but only just."

The adjutant raised his eyebrows, nodded and went away. We fell silent again. Hawkins came back from Shrapnel Valley and passed us. I thought he was staring at Ned, but it seemed he didn't see him.

The doctor said, "Better get under cover, Hawkins."

Hawkins curled up in his dugout.

Presently the waiting was over. Death had won — for Ned, the last trench was taken, the final fortress stormed.

CHAPTER
TEN

THE "GALLOPER" WITHOUT A HORSE

Day and night, night and day came and went like the pendulum of an eternal clock. The days grew into weeks and ushered in the first breath of summer.

So much had happened from the day we landed at Anzac Cove and that first wonderful rush up the slopes. But our footing on the peninsula was now secure. Trenches were deep, reasonably safe, and numerous. Communications with our support trenches, where reinforcements rested, were well established. Our guns were in position, every man had his own dugout. The Army had increased, populating the wilderness.

Our field artillery brigade had moved headquarters from the beach to a hillock near the head of Shrapnel Valley. The change left us nearer the firing line. Several more of our fellows had landed and the Brigade Staff was nearly complete again.

Much of our desert training had been for nothing, as we had landed hardly a horse ashore and mules performed all the transport and the mountain battery work. The guns were manhandled to their respective positions and then dug in. Heavy sandbagged ramparts grew around the guns and an overhead cover of more sandbags went up. And there the guns stayed for days, sometimes even for weeks.

In spite of all our hard work bringing a large number of horses from Australia they had all been returned to Egypt. The result was that the haughtiest generals had to tramp around like common soldiers. And among the hapless horsemen left horseless to toil the hills on foot was Gunner Lake. I remained "Galloper Lake" in name only, and instead of galloping I had to carry messages or walk behind the colonel on each and every excursion he made. Because the colonel was restless as the wind, I became known as "The Periscope Carrier".

Our signal practice was also wasted — from first to last we never waved a flag; all lines of communication were kept by telephonists. The signallers sat down to office duties. Staff telephonists made a large dugout, with seats and a step down. All lines came together there, so that the place grew into a regular exchange with switchboards and other affairs. You would always find two or three fellows "at home" here, with a heap of old Melbourne newspapers in the corner. These fellows were ever ready for a yarn and could give you beach information in return for trench news.

Lieutenant Sands, officer of many duties, was employed as the forward observer for the artillery in another attack, our third attempt to capture the village of Krithia. We did not see him for two or three days and then he suddenly appeared from the wilderness in a piteous condition. He was covered with red dust, unshaven and unwashed, his clothes were crumpled and torn and one of his boots had lost its heel. His nose was running and he had the look of a man far gone with hunger and thirst.

I was not doing anything in particular when he turned up, so I kept an eye on him. Despite my initial antipathy to him, I liked the fellow, and he was no coward.

He found scant welcome here. The colonel spoke a few words to him and then dismissed him with an abrupt nod. The other officers said nothing at all.

Sands sat down without a word and emptied somebody's water bottle. After midday tucker Sands perked up — once again he became the egotistical officer. He found a handkerchief somewhere and then came over in my direction and sat down affably enough and smiled.

"You're still alive?" he said, looking at the ground. He picked a leaf from a bush and crumpled it in his hand.

"Yes, sir, I'm all right."

Sands did not look directly at me, a trait I had often noticed in him. While crumpling the leaf to powder he said, "How do you like it here?"

"It's better than training at Mena Camp."

Sands gave a low chuckle.

I continued, "What sort of time have you had, sir?"

He still said nothing, but laughed again. I persisted, "You were over here pretty early, weren't you, sir?"

"Oh, yes, Lake, pretty early," he answered. "But I wasn't in the rush up the hill. I was with the brigadier."

178

"The infantry seem to have done all right," I said. "You can see their packs at the bottom of the hill over there, where they threw them off."

"Yes, the Third Battalion did well," Sands went on, after a pause. "But you know it wasn't the great affair it was meant to be. We were expected to land lower down, on flat land. But there was some mistake or other and we were put off here. The Turkish Army was lower down and there was only a machine gun detachment on the beach. After they had been rushed, there was practically no resistance until we were at the top of the hill. By then the Turks had brought their men up and when we got to the open country we came under fire — our men began to waver and fall back. That's why so many officers were lost, rallying them. Afterwards they advanced too far and pushed on almost into the Turkish camp. The promised reinforcements never landed, so they had to retreat under heavy fire and so the losses happened."

We had been told that our victory over the Turks was great, but Sands's story was the more likely one. The lieutenant took up his tale again.

"The battalions lost themselves that first day. They were all mixed up, and until there is a chance to reorganise a bit, thousands more will be missing."

We sat a long time without speaking. At last Sands looked sideways at me.

"Lake, next time you are down at the beach, do you think you could find me a pair of boots? Mine are done for."

With that he showed me the boot with the heel gone. "You ought to be able to get a pair at the hospital or the morgue. One boot will do if you can't get a pair."

He looked so broken and said so little of his troubles that my heart went out to him. I answered that I'd do what I could.

Next morning I was passing the field hospital and, remembering Sands's request, looked inside. The picture was not pleasant and there seemed no boots about. So I went to the quartermaster, and after a little haggling, I got a new pair. Away I started, and on my return I dangled them in front of Sands.

"You've got a new pair!" he exclaimed, getting up in a hurry. "You're the most wonderful man, Lake. I never could have got them."

"I couldn't get any laces, sir," I said, amazed at the change in the man.

"Doesn't matter. They're splendid. I would willingly give ten shillings for them."

And so our old enmity was buried.

In a couple of weeks the whole face of the peninsula had changed. The scrub was thinning under the demands of firewood, roads pierced the main valleys and linked them together, while paths crawled over the hills wherever there were headquarters or gunpits. Our men dug tunnels close to the Turkish lines while the Turks were digging close to ours, tap-tapping away so near to us that at times we could hear them. The feeling of great adventure was over and there was nothing to do but endure and hope to survive to the end. But by now we all realised that our chances of survival were slim.

Springtime had come and amorous birds played hide-and-seek through all this ruin. Whenever the guns shut their mouths you could hear the birds singing.

I had a central dugout near Brigade Headquarters and the cookhouse. From the seat inside it I could look across the sea into the eye of the setting sun. A tiny path, just above my dugout, was used by everyone coming from the valley top to headquarters. Invariably, those who passed sent a trickle of dirt into my bed. Some spadework might have alleviated the problem, but I was too lazy to undertake such hard work.

A sad-looking bush grew by the path, but I received no shade from it. So I was obliged to rig a shaky overhead covering of tarpaulins, which kept the sun off part of the time. But when there was no breeze, the space underneath the cover became sickly hot. At night I took it down so I could watch the stars moving in the sky; while leaning on one elbow I could also look out over the sea.

There was plenty to eat, so we were always certain of our dinner, although the food was uninteresting and at times almost inedible. A fatigue party of batmen made daily trips to the beach for rations. And so, like all the others of the Brigade Staff, I settled down to the humdrum of everyday affairs.

From Walker's Ridge to The Wheatfield the colonel and I knew the winding of every trench. In an instant I could up-end the periscope and point it to whatever the colonel wanted to look at: Lone Pine,[32] Jackson's

181

[Johnston's] Jolly, Collins Street or The Chessboard. And I could point to the hidden battery at C and show the puff of the gun on Turk's Hump.

In the beginning our guns had little luck — truth to tell, they were at a disadvantage. The country was certainly not a field gunner's terrain. As we lacked the horses we had to move the guns by means of imprecations and sweat. Also, the lay of the country was wrong, and space so lacking that we had to shoot from the pockets of our own infantrymen. This attracted enemy fire on neighbouring trenches, and accordingly, the infantry hated us.

Colonel Jackson was a restless spirit, loving the company of his guns. First thing each day he would make his bath in a spoonful of water, standing up naked as the ground below and rubbing himself briskly. After the bath he had a shave, and while he dressed he talked over the telephone to Divisional Artillery or the batteries.

Then we began our rounds. The colonel would get up, tuck the periscope under his arm with a "Come along, Lake" and lead the way up the path above my dugout. I followed close on his heels. A few yards on he would hand me the periscope without turning around or saying a word.

Most of the time the colonel said nothing at all. Level country or hilly land, he went at an eager pace. Each morning we went the same way, starting on B Battery preserve and ending there again at midday or later.

The steep, sloping path above my dugout led to the head of Shrapnel Valley. It was one of the two main valleys that pierced the hills — the other one was Monash Valley.

Shrapnel Valley was the centre of our position. Initially the whole valley had been a vast wilderness, but it was not long before the sappers had tapped there for water and a couple of barrels appeared halfway up. About the same time a field dressing station came into being in the area. As the position was strategically important, our Infantry Brigade Headquarters claimed the top of the valley; a New South Wales Battalion Headquarters kept house alongside. We gunners prospected lower down the slope. Cookhouses and dugouts for officers came in our wake, and in no time a primitive township grew up, with suburbs wandering downhill towards the beach.

As often as not the colonel made his first call at Infantry Brigade Headquarters, which we had to pass on the way. I read the Reuter's telegrams from a notice board outside while the colonel went inside to see the infantry brigadier, General Runner.[33]

The general was a tough customer and, judging from his ribbons and the colour of his face, an Indian Army man. His ADC was trained to jump at the wrinkle of an eyelid or the bristle of a moustache hair. What his staff thought of General Runner I don't know, but the men liked him well enough. He had a curious droop of an eyelid and seemed to shut his eyes when darting a savage glance at you. I suspect Runner had a bad liver, and I was sorry for his batman.

183

The general was forever poking about the trenches, and he was not wary of risk. He was a true periscope fiend, holding the instrument well above the parapet so that every sniper for hundreds of yards was potting away at it. Possibly periscope casualties were his vanity.

One morning the periscope was struck sideways. The general's head was just below the parapet and the bullet passed an inch or so over his cap. He cocked his eye up — he had quick movements, like a bird — and looked at the holes in the tin case.

"Bullet through the periscope, sir?" came a mocking voice. The general chuckled and continued his observation.

Whenever Colonel Jackson and I made an early call at Infantry Brigade Headquarters, General Runner would be at breakfast or in his office. He had built a table of a sort and sat at the head of it, often in the open air, with his staff in front of him. Although there was nothing special to eat, the company lived in a civilised fashion.

On the colonel's approach, the general would look up. "Good morning, Jackson," he would say, passing a hand over his hair in that special way of his. Then he would wrinkle his face and squint, for the sun was always in his eyes.

"Morning, sir."

Then the two officers would talk for a few minutes, the general in a strong high-pitched voice. Runner always had the last word. He had strange artillery ideas and, apparently, it was hard to make him change his mind. However, argument and explanation did not delay his breakfast. He chewed with easy indifference. Then we would depart, the colonel often not pleased with the outcome of their conversation.

We would start up a very steep slope, which took us to the top of the valley. There the trenches ran to the right and left, with the dry watercourse in between. This gap was protected by wire entanglements and sandbag ramparts.

Once we dragged a couple of guns behind these trenches, but we had no luck with them. Two sergeants were sniped before a shot was fired. Afterwards the guns went back to the bottom of the valley and stayed there, against the wishes of the colonel.

Near the top of the valley were some well-constructed dugouts, places where plenty of sawn timber had been used and with roofs of corrugated iron and sandbags — curtains of old sacking kept the sun out. There were always rough tables in such places and plenty of up-ended packing cases for chairs. One could tell a man's character from the condition of his funk-hole.

In the creek bed was a cookhouse where a cook concocted savoury dishes from pretty hopeless ingredients.

On a red-hot afternoon I sat on the bank above the cookhouse, wondering how he found the spirit to continue with his work. Over time the cook had grown a beard, but he never left it to straggle as some of the other men did. It was neatly pointed and trimmed. He talked to nobody. Maybe he cooked to forget his

185

miseries. He cooked and he kept his mouth shut, which was all that was asked of him.

A sergeant in charge of trench mortars lived among bombs and empty boxes in a nearby dugout. He was a small, middle-aged man with sad eyes. He was a real gentleman and was said to have a history.

At the head of the valley we had to turn right to reach B Battery observing station or left to Clayton's trenches, where Sands had his observation post. We always turned to the right. Our path ran through a deep cutting with scooped-out seats on either side. Stretcher-bearers would sit there, reading papers or playing cards. Other fellows sat there as well, gambling for cigarettes while enjoying the few yards of shade and the slight draught caused by the high walls.

Beyond the gamblers the trenches started with the entrance to B Battery observing station nearby. The spot was much improved since Marines had held it; now it was wider, as the enemy had lost interest in it. The telephonists sweltered in the sun, as there was not a spot of shade. More often than not the battery commander, Major Cannister, was with his men.

I remember one particular visit to the observing station, when the colonel was in a rather pensive mood.

"Good morning, Cannister," the colonel said on arrival, glad to catch his breath after the steep climb.

The officers saluted one another.

"Morning, sir," Cannister said and moved away from the big periscope tied against the parapet, leaving the sergeant-major to watch in his place. Side by side the two officers sat down on the hot earth and exchanged the latest news.

The colonel opened his cigarette case and cast a bitter eye on the weekly ration of Woodbines.

"Have one?" he asked the major, holding the case open for him. "I'm getting some real cigarettes this week, thank God!" The colonel took one himself, lit it while staring thoughtfully at the opposite wall of the dugout.

After a while he asked, "Anything doing this morning, Cannister?"

"Nothing really — I put a round into C half an hour ago, that's all."

"Careful, Cannister, we can't afford to throw away a single round. We're cut down to five rounds this morning. Five rounds a day! Good God! And this is supposed to be a war!"

"Short of ammunition again?" asked Cannister.

"Yes, and after all the talk. The old man rang me up this morning and said five was our limit. He had done all he could, but it was no use. They're saving up for something. We're going to have a real battle in a day or two, with noise and smoke and two or three extra rounds to fire off. It should mean a column in *The Argus* for us. Think of it, Cannister!"

Cannister crossed his legs and smiled, but said nothing. However, the colonel had enough talk for two.

Impatiently he went on: "If we're not allowed to fight, why for Heaven's sake do they bring us here? One might just as well be in Melbourne, where one could get a drink and some decent cigarettes. How much ammunition has arrived with the new howitzers, do you think? Fifty rounds, that's all! Good God! Why don't we shoot off all we've got, pack up the guns and send them home, and go to Hell like gentlemen!"

Cannister did not reply. The colonel continued: "The brigadier has started fussing again. I don't know what he expects us to do. He's on again about the Turkish gun at Mortar Ridge. I've told him a dozen times it's a New Zealand target. God knows what those New Zealanders are doing! They never open their mouths, or if they do they shut them again at the first return shell."

So the talk went on and on until it was time to leave.

Then the colonel took a final look through the periscope I had carried for him. "I'm going to C Battery and then to A. Ring me up if you want me."

Colonel and major saluted. I shouldered the periscope and we marched off through the trenches, making good time along less crowded sections. We often pulled up to look at some of the Turkish handiwork from this or that position, or stopped to gather the latest news or to pass the time of day.

Some may regard a trench as a romantic place, but it makes a thankless home. Most trenches were deep and narrow, safe from rifle fire and pretty secure from shrapnel. Nevertheless, accidents did occur. A fellow would keep his head too far above the parapet or look too long through a peephole and get sniped.

Sometimes a bullet penetrated a badly filled sandbag and settled some poor devil's account. Then the call would come: "Pass the word for stretcher-bearers." The men gambling near the entrance would spring into action and hurry along. There would be a few minutes' delay when a dead man was wrapped up in a blanket or waterproof sheet and put on the stretcher, with his pack and other belongings. Then the stretcher-bearers would start the tiring journey to the beach.

Someone would get hold of a shovel and cover up the bloodstain — and that was the end of the affair. You might hear them say: "Smith's gone. Bad luck, wasn't it? Bullet copped 'im in the 'ead. 'E wasn't a bad bloke."

Sun, thirst, indifferent food and lack of sleep left little energy for regret.

The trenches zig-zagged all the way, so enemy fire could not enfilade for any distance. The sun stared down onto the baked earth and searched out every corner. To provide some shade, fellows stretched blankets overhead, pinned to the walls with bayonets. Sometimes attempts were made to get little comforts, such as seats, little fireplaces, shelves for ammunition, rifle racks dug out of the wall and pictures from illustrated papers. But nothing really disguised the horror of these homes. You could not make space where there was no space, you could not blot out the sun; nor could you make nectar of stewed tea, nor a banquet from Army rations. You could not charm away the flies that descended in hosts, nor pretend you had no use for Keating's Flea Powder.

One could push up the periscope and stare upon the strangest, stillest scene: a stretch of barren heathland, bearing such poor bushes and herbs as the pitiless sun allowed. One could catch sight of a field of rusty browns and faded greens, with here and there brighter spots where hardy heath flowers blossomed. It was like peering into some magic world, far remote from our everyday existence.

Death was the farmer of that tranquil field. Look at the corpses, tumbled over in every shape, as still as still could be. Mark the green uniforms holding the sunlight, and the dusky faces, hideously misshapen with decay. Mark the swollen bodies. Mark the rotting eye sockets. By night and by day shells pass over them, but this silent company sleeps on.

We came one morning to a new post that lay beyond our beat. There the dead lay thickly spread and the stench was sickening. The week before a charge had swept over that terrain and up to the very muzzles of our rifles. Bodies lay within a few yards of the parapet.

I twisted the periscope this way and that to get a better view. Suddenly I saw a dead Turk right in front of me, so near that it was difficult to get him in full view of the periscope. I made an opening between the sandbags and looked at him face to face. The Turk had crawled up all the way, but at the last moment one of our men had fired point blank and killed him. In the centre of his forehead was a black hole. He had made no further movement; it was obvious he had died immediately. Now his corpse was blackening and swelling as the fierce sun poured over him. He would swell and swell and his clothes would flap wearily whenever a wind passed by, and rust spots would creep up his rifle.

Surely, far away some woman had been praying to Allah for his safe return. To die at the rim of your enemy's trench with your rifle at your side, a soldier may regard as a fair end. I filled in the crack between the sandbags and stepped down again onto the trench floor.

Many times one could pass through the trenches without a sign of war other than men polishing their rifles. One would find men shaving, men cooking little dinners, men reading old newspapers or writing love letters, while others were sleeping. Some were naked to the waist, hunting for body lice among the seams and crevices of their shirts.

One might come across fatigue parties, armed with spades and sandbags, who were strengthening the parapets, building new traverses or digging tunnels towards the enemy. Members of such parties were all dirt and sweat, but at the end of the day there was no washing for them. All they could do was pull on their shirts and lie back, trying to forget their misery in a dog's doze.

Grumbling was rife. I heard men pray for a bullet to end their lives. There were mysterious accidents, such as bullet through the hand, the trigger finger or the foot. Yet all the time there was heart in us still. There were men eager to tell what they had done before being foolish enough to join this affair. Others were ready to tell you what they were going to do after they returned home. Everywhere there was conviction that we would have the final victory.

But it was not always peaceful in the trenches. The enemy would take fits of rage and shell us mercilessly. We hardly minded when they sent ordinary shrapnel, but in the course of time big guns were brought up, which was a very different matter. There was always an evening battle. And then came the big attacks, which is another story.

Other units had observing stations along here — the New Zealanders had one, and the Indian gunners another. Passing them the colonel and I would always stop for a little yarn.

The Indian soldiers were friendly fellows. Once we met a white officer and two or three native telephonists.

"Good day, sir."

"Good day."

We saluted each other and came to a standstill.

"Anything special going on?" the colonel asked.

"They're making a great work of Lone Pine — hard at it all morning. Something ought to be done before it gets too strong."

Out came the colonel's hand for the periscope. "Yes," he said after breaking off from a long look. "Lone Pine and the Jolly are too strong for my liking, and too near. Something should be done right away. The places are little fortresses stuck right under our nose."

The colonel looked again and then turned round. "I suppose you know we knocked that gun out yesterday?"

"We claim that, sir. But I hear the New Zealanders said they did it."

"They claim that, do they? What damned cheek! It was ours, for sure. The Turks had the gun out in the open — you could see the gunners standing up to it breast high. We put a shell right on top of it and left it on its side. Look, it's there now."

The colonel took another look round the landscape. "They've got a road over there, quite a thoroughfare. Mules and camels pass up and down all day. I might give them a bit of a hurry-up. Probably when they're having afternoon tea. A round or two would be just the thing."

The Indian officer replied, "You might plug one right into the band."

"Quite so. Quite so. By the way, we have been cut down again — five rounds per day is the limit now. I wonder why we bothered to come here. Soon we'll be told that we're out of ammunition altogether. Then I'll have to throw my glasses at them or hit them over the head with the periscope."

Then the colonel resumed his staring into the periscope. "I'll have to put a round into that road today on the way home. It'll be dinner time then. They'll be out in the open and there will be a better chance to catch somebody. Besides, it will mean a spoilt dinner, if nothing else."

We pushed on towards C Battery, located on a rise we called The Pimple. A few more traverses and a few more turnings brought us there. A couple of guns were level with the trenches and the others were some two hundred yards further back. The trench guns had a sturdy overhead cover of sandbags and a sandbag

193

screen in front. The surroundings were more open and not so precipitous; it was less miserable to live here. The battery commander had built himself a good dugout: a square, fairly roomy place, where he passed the day when nothing important was on hand. He had an epicure's soul and, being a wise man, he got himself as good a living as possible. His meals were always more tempting than ours. The colonel knew it and broke his journey there on many a scorching morning.

I am sure that in his heart the colonel longed for Melbourne's gourmet dishes. "Yards is a very poor housekeeper," I heard him say many times, shaking his head sadly. At this the commander would laugh. He was a stout man with a ruddy complexion, which matched the red ribbon of the Distinguished Service Order he wore on his coat.

It was relatively quiet around The Pimple, as most of the enemy fire passed over into the open country beyond. Nevertheless, one day a shell just missed me, striking a bank only inches overhead and bursting upwards.

Further along you entered an open valley overlooking the sea. No doubt it had once been covered in scrub like the other hillsides, but a rest camp had grown up here and the place was now riddled with funk-holes, communication trenches and cookhouses. I don't know why the spot was chosen, because it was poorly sheltered. During one period it underwent heavy daily doses of shellfire.

To reach A Battery one had to cross the area and more open country beyond. A fairly good road led there, taking you past a graveyard on the right. There were still some bushes among the graves where a few of the remaining tits and goldfinches sheltered. Later on they too flew away. The road sloped steeply towards the sea, and not far down it a footpath ran off to A Battery.

One hazy morning the colonel and I were coming back from A Battery. We reached the end of the footpath where it joined the road. Shrapnel was falling down the valley in generous style, and those unlucky enough to be on business there spent as little time on their errands as possible.

The colonel sat down on the bank to cool off and allow the Turkish gunners to tire. As the situation remained unaltered after five minutes, he stood up again. While humping his shoulders and stroking his nose with the periscope he looked up the valley towards the C Battery dugouts. Suddenly the colonel cried out, "Lake! Watch out! Run!"

We both ran as fast as we could before a shell turned the place we had been occupying into a crater.

CHAPTER
ELEVEN

THE BURIAL OF THREE THOUSAND CORPSES

Sooner or later you would meet all the celebrities poking round in the trenches. At one time General Rivers[34] came daily to The Pimple, smoking a cigarette in a long thin holder. He had a favourite seat beside one of C Battery guns. He was tall and thin, with a slight stoop as I remember, and, for a soldier, an air of great refinement. His hands were white, with long fingers and nails so clean he might have walked off Collins Street or Mayfair. He sat and smoked silently, or walked up and down, pointing quietly with his head. I don't know how he treated his staff, but he seemed reasonable enough in his dealings with us.

Another man I conducted through the trenches more than once was Captain Carrot, the war correspondent. He was tall and thin, with a peaky face and glasses. He carried a camera in place of a rifle and got around a great deal. In Egypt he had written an article about troops being sent home for disorderly conduct, which had greatly offended some senior officers. Someone told me that later, in a charge at Cape Helles, Captain Carrot had bravely come out in the open in full sight of the Turks. And so he was forgiven. I don't know how true the story was. Carrot had little to say to me.[35]

Another celebrity who frequently ran to earth in our trenches was Colonel Saxon VC. He was a quiet man with a polished manner and a lisp. I heard he came from a crack English regiment. He often left his staff behind and poked about on his own, periscope under his arm. He was never put out and took it all as part of a day's happenings in war.

"Birdwood is awfully angry with me this morning," Saxon lisped to Colonel Jackson when we ran into him on one morning's round. "I don't know what I've done. I thought I had better go for a walk while he cools down. Everything's quite dead today. I'm off to Quinn's Post."[36]

And last, but very far from least, on some fine morning General Birdwood strolled round the corner with his ADC, his periscope bearer, his map-case bearer and all the following of a mighty man of war. He was a popular commander. As often as not his dress was a sun helmet, a plain khaki shirt, corduroy knickerbockers and leggings cut after the style of an English squire or well-to-do yeoman. He carried a walking stick in his hand. He was usually calm and easygoing. His face showed good temper, but there was a strong chin at the bottom of it. The general looked like a man who would haul you off, swing a fist and lay you out rather than put you under arrest. He spoke to all and sundry in the trenches and bathed freely with the men in the sea, all of whom were naked.

I stood beside General Birdwood once at the head of Shrapnel Gully when he had a near miss from a Turkish sniper.

"Now, where's that rascal?" the general said, lifting up his head. "Can't any of you men get rid of him? We ought not to allow that." One or other of his ADCs followed at his heels and brigadiers and lesser fry swelled the train, until one had to push against the trench wall to let the procession go by.

The men in A Battery were to be envied, because their views were the finest anywhere on the peninsula. They had a broad view of the blue sea and could gaze at the impregnable hill of Achi Baba, which was down below and not far away. It ran into the sea, shaped like a man's finger. One could see the ruined observing station and the wire entanglements.

On our visits to A Battery we were often in awe of the stunning panorama. Some mornings the sea was calm and the fleets were all asleep. Other mornings the battleships lay off Achi Baba, hurling vast shells onto the ridges. You could hear the rumbling and watch the cones of dust rise into the skies.

From a wide ledge outside the first communication trench was the best view of all. From there one morning the colonel and I sighted the *Albion* run aground. She had run onto a mudbank in a submarine scare. Gaba Tepe peppered away with might and a battleship in the straits tossed huge shells across the peninsula. Round the unhappy boat fussed the *Canopus*, trying to pull her off the bank with hawsers.

As our watch ended, the *Albion* finally managed to slip away.

"There she goes!" burst out the colonel, putting away his glasses. "There she scuttles away like a . . . No, I better not mention the word!"

Already I have told you of the flat country dividing us from Achi Baba. In daytime it was revealed as rich and cultivated land, broken by lines of trees. It looked as though it was a home for shepherdesses and lovesick piping shepherds. But that was an illusion, because in an olive grove towards the far side there lurked a huge gun named Beachy Bill. By day and by night the gun waited there, preying upon the beach and the anchorage. Incredible numbers of deaths were attributed to it, and one unlucky afternoon its pellets grazed my own back.

Beachy Bill had a comrade in arms, the Anafarta gun, which fired from Anafarta, the low land beyond and to our left. Either gun would sweep the beach at all hours of the day. You took your life in your own hands if you dared leave the shelter of the provision stacks. The big guns would snipe at the crowds around the water tanks and at the bathers in the sea. The guns would send sandbags flying into the dugouts and scatter the cheeses and the biscuit cases. They were the scourge of all who dwelt on the beach.

In spite of their idyllic view, the men of A Battery enjoyed very few peaceful hours. The enemy knew their whereabouts with accuracy. The moment they opened their mouths to eat, half a dozen shells would tear over. Through that long summer many stretchers made the journey to the beach. The gunners who did survive grew leaner and more suntanned and swore more heartfelt oaths.

One afternoon I met Little Billy Blake in the valley.

"Have you heard about poor Bill Eaves?" Billy asked.

"No."

"Shot dead," Billy said.

"Damn sorry to hear that," I said, remembering my conversations with Eaves in our camp at Cairo. "How did it happen?"

"Dunno. They found him at the top of the valley. A bit of shrapnel copped him in the top of the head. His eyes were hanging out of his head like cricket balls. I helped to take him down to the beach. 'Struth, was I sweating by the time we got there!"

"Bad luck for poor old Bill," I said.

"Blasted bad luck," said Blake.

Then Billy Blake continued down the valley and I climbed up the hill to headquarters.

As a rule, the colonel would return to headquarters after completing our morning rounds and I would see no more of him for several hours. Then my time was my own, so I crawled under the wretched awning of my funk-hole in the heat of the day and settled down to be grilled. My only hope was that the water supply would last until nightfall, so I could go down to the beach for more.

By three or four o'clock the colonel would come to life again and emerge in the open. After collecting his periscope and glasses he would call out, "Come on,

Lake!" and up we went along the path up to the valley's head. Occasionally we went up the left trench, passing an observing station that came under Sands's jurisdiction.

Every afternoon, at four or five o'clock, or even later, we had our evening battle. Through much of the day, when even the flies fell exhausted into the tea, the snipers of either side lost heart. In the heat of the day the gunners lay by their guns, wondering why they had not died yet. However, as the sun went down and a flagging breeze puffed off the sea, we rose again to our feet, picked up periscopes and telephones and forced ourselves into another round of evening hatred. At that time of the day we asked for trouble, putting in a round here and a round there until we got our target.

At this time — late spring — the Turkish army conducted a mighty effort to drive us into the sea. We were told that Turkish newspapers called it "purging the beach of our presence".

In early summer the Turks launched a major attack along the entire front. At the end of several fierce hours the attempt was spent, and the enemy reeled to their trenches, leaving on a few acres of ground almost four thousand corpses. Everywhere you looked the dead men lay. Hours later you might see an arm move or a leg rise, where some poor fellow cried on Death not to delay. In time the breath of decay searched out the length of Shrapnel Valley, and whenever the wind veered in the trenches, the stench caught at our throats.

One evening, on the heels of the big attack, we had a pretty little battle. The colonel observed from B Battery station and I carried orders to the telephonist a few yards away.

The major had not turned up and Lieutenant Hay was in charge. B Battery was dusting up what we had named Collins Street, or one of the other targets, and the other batteries banged away elsewhere with more than the daily dose of hate. A great many snipers were at work on either side.

The great heat of the day had passed, and indeed there were signs of evening. The sun was three parts of the way down the sky and shadows started to grow at the bottom of every bush. With the noon heat haze gone, you could see with clarity over the desolate countryside. Our shells burst in white clouds on the great hill in the distance and here and there were the puffs of the enemy's return fire. And nearer at hand, you could follow the Turkish trenches from the vicious dust spurts of our bullets.

Where the colonel took his stand, they were tunnelling out a machine gun position, and every few moments men came out of the earth with freshly-filled sandbags on their shoulders. They crowded the narrow passage, blocking me every time I hurried to Hay or the telephonist who had replaced Bill Eaves.

The colonel stood on a platform, head just under the parapet, periscope just above. His size caused him to crouch, and his legs were wide apart. The brisker the battle grew, the more engrossed he became. He never moved his head, but stayed bending forward staring into the glass, exclaiming at intervals, "That's a good one! Very good! Right on the target that was!"

"That's pretty shooting! Green's into 'em now!"

"Damn it! They're off! Are you there, Lake?"

I was below, watching for the least sign, for often a movement of the hand was his only signal or he would jerk out an abrupt word or two.

Now I answered, "Yes, sir," and stood ready.

"Tell Hay to come over more. Two degrees more right. That's better, that's better! He can come over further. Two degrees more to the right. Tell him that!"

Away I ran with his command.

Lieutenant Hay was at the periscope and nodded to show he had heard me.

As I moved off again, he called out: "Tell the colonel they seem to be waving flags over there to attract attention. They were doing it before. Now they've started again."

I told the colonel what he had said, but got no answer for my pains. I would have looked myself had there been time.

"That's better, that's better!" the colonel started to say. "Now he's short! Damn it, he's short! Lake, tell him to add fifty. Say he wants fifty or a hundred."

I took the message and ran back again, finding time to sit down for a moment.

The action continued, losing little or nothing of its briskness. Then came word down the line, passed in a mysterious unofficial way, that something was happening on the other side; the enemy was waving flags and looking over the parapets, as if to attract attention.

But it seemed no more was to come of it. Firing continued and the moment's excitement was spent.

Yet five minutes later it had grown again. We thought something must happen now. I itched to see how matters went, but I could not leave the spot. The firing lost heart, becoming a number of sharp explosions in place of an unbroken roll.

Again the word came along. The colonel took interest finally and stopped a passing officer to inquire and then looked again at the opposite trenches. Finally he gave word for the batteries to cease their fire and stepped down onto the floor of the trench. I lost no time picking up a periscope and seeing all there was to see. It was little enough. The enemy must have given up their idea, for not one flag flew. I soon tired and sat down on a ledge belonging to some machine gunners who had the habit of sleeping through the day and coming out to fire in the evening. Each man had a recess of his own with a blanket hung before it to cheat the sun. Their legs remained in sight, so I knew them better by their feet than their faces.

By the time I sat down again the colonel had disappeared. Maybe he went to pass the time of day with an infantry colonel whose dugout was a few steps down the path. Often he did this, leaving me in the trench to call him if need be. Just now there were several sets of legs showing beyond the blankets and there was an argument.

"I joined up fer the six bob entry commission, of course. What else would a bloke do it fer?"

"I joined 'cos I 'ad a row with the old woman. I went out in an 'urry and joined up right away. And now I bloody well wish I 'adn't."

"What did you join fer, Darkie? Was it the six bob, a row with yer tart or was the police after yer?"

Darkie, an Aboriginal soldier, made no answer.

"What was it, Darkie?"

"I joined cos I thought a bloke ought ter join."

His words had the force equal to an 8.25 shell. Nobody said anything. Nobody moved at all. I looked around for a museum to put such a sentiment in.

We were wide awake this afternoon as brisk rifle fire continued. I sat where I was, hearing the noise and yet not hearing it. The sun was setting, a few shadows spread about and there was even a suggestion of evening cool. But the place still had the power to destroy one mentally and morally.

Then without warning someone yelled, "They're waving flags again."

"There's something doing! There's something up!"

I got up with a yawn and went to the parapet and poked up the periscope. Straight in front of me was a big white flag charged with a red crescent, moving slowly forwards and backwards over the enemy parapet. As I watched, a second one rose up on our right, and at odd intervals appeared streamers, which might have been small flags or even rags.

Around me anyone who could get hold of a periscope tried to find out what was happening.

I had taken stand among the B Battery men, beside their periscope. The parapet was quite low and it took little effort to look over the top. I debated whether to take the risk and see at first hand how matters went. There was movement in the enemy's trench beside the

205

largest flag. Suddenly a man climbed over the parapet and dropped onto the open ground. For a moment he stood still in uneasy fashion, then he came forward, holding the big white flag with the red crescent overhead.

I felt like crying out in admiration.

Our snipers shot yet in scores, in hundreds maybe. At any moment a stray shot or the aimed one of some fool might tumble him over. And no one knew the danger better than he himself, for he bowed his head and upper body as does a man advancing in the teeth of a great wind. He came forward with deliberate steps, moving his flag in wide semicircles.

"To the devil with caution," I said and stood up and looked across the open. "By Jove!" I called out. Beside me was Lieutenant Hay, wondering whether I had gone mad.

News had travelled everywhere that something special was on hand, for cries went up and down: "Cease fire there! Cease fire!"

And the firing did die away, though unwillingly, lessening and returning again in gusts.

Meanwhile the man of peace continued on his way. Maybe before starting on the journey, he had delivered his soul into Allah's safekeeping, for no shot touched him and it seemed no fear could turn him from his path. This moved me as I looked at his unhurried pace and the slow waving of his flag. My heart cried out to him. "I salute you, friend. A brave man's heart is crying out to a brave man!"

206

When the man of peace had advanced halfway, the rifle fire of both sides was nearly silent and there was a stir of uncertainty in our ranks. You heard some crying, "Cease fire," while others called out that no order had been given and what the devil was everyone on about.

But the firing did not start again, or only in short-lived bursts. The men hung by the peepholes, waiting to see what might befall. There was a stir on our side, near Clayton's trench it seemed. Soon an officer came into the open, with a handkerchief tied to a stick or a rifle, I could not see which. At the same time a couple of Turks appeared from their trenches, and another of our men went forward; it seemed they would hold a party then and there. While I looked to see, I found the colonel at my shoulder.

"Get the interpreter, Lake," he said. "Quickly, get Bargi and bring him here. He may be wanted."

I went over the top to the telephonist and sent down word. Then I came back again and informed the colonel. Next I jumped onto the parapet once more to look over the country.

The little company had come together some hundreds of yards away and were in parley, but I could not hear what was said. I grew eager for Bargi's coming and cursed him for his slowness.

Then a second big flag was put up to our right. Two men jumped into the open and came towards our trenches, one empty-handed and one carrying the flag.

The colonel looked round sharply and made moves to go over there, then suddenly turned to me and asked impatiently, "Where's Bargi, Lake?"

"He's on the way, sir."

"Meet him and hurry him up. Say I want him at once!"

I pushed towards the trench mouth as speedily as could be managed, not very eager for another run down the hill and back again. But at the turn of the trench I met Bargi, with sweat on his face. He was blowing with his exertions and had a look half-pleased, half-scared.

Bargi was an Italian Jew from Trieste who spoke and wrote a dozen languages. By trade he had been a photographer. When war was declared, times grew hard, and he had made up his mind to go soldiering. But he mistook his new vocation, because he was the most cowardly man in the entire brigade.

"My disposition is very nervous," he said, shrugging his shoulders deprecatingly. "I'm too sensitive."

"Sensitive! My friend, we call it by another name," I thought. Despite his cowardice, I was sorry for the man.

He asked me what was wanted.

"The colonel wants you in a hurry. He is waiting a few yards up the trench."

No more was said. Bargi went on without more speech, and I turned to follow. Lewis, who had guided Bargi up here, pulled at my sleeve and asked what was happening.

"There's a bit of an armistice on," I called out as I turned. "Have a look for yourself. I have to get after the colonel." I left Lewis standing in the middle of the path, his hands in his pockets and a silly stare on his face. Lewis may have been a pretty fellow, but he was a rank bore.

The couple of seconds' delay had lost me Bargi, so I did my best to catch up with him before he met the colonel and they would then disappear together. Fortune nodded, and I saw their heels rounding a traverse, enabling me to link up with them within seconds. The colonel moved in great hurry through the almost empty trench, and fat little Bargi, who was still out of breath, had trouble keeping up with him. Sometimes Bargi threw timid glances at me, for it was his first trench journey and truly he was receiving a brusque introduction.

Presently it became more crowded again and we had to slow our pace. Next we met a crossroad, which brought us to a standstill. After someone put us onto the right track we started anew to elbow forward. Finally we had come as far as was possible. The colonel put up his periscope to find where we were and I jumped up onto a platform and poked my head over the parapet. We could hear the crack of a rifle now and again, but not often.

We had come to the best spot. The men with the flag were right opposite. They were nearer than before, yet they had not come over all the way. At that moment they still looked undecidedly in our direction. I do not doubt they cared little for their exposed position.

Almost at once Bargi climbed up beside me so the three of us stood side by side. The colonel looked into the periscope and Bargi stood on tiptoe, peeping over the parapet. The two Turks continued to hesitate — in fact they even made a motion of retreat. "Call them, Bargi!" the colonel burst out. "Tell them to come on, say it's all right!"

The little man looked anxiously about, but pulled himself together and called out something in Turkish. However, his words failed to carry all the way, so he clasped hands to his mouth and cried out anew, this time at the top of his voice. At once the Turks were reassured; they scanned the trenches eagerly to find the voice. After an exchange of a sentence or two they came forward deliberately, one man bearing the standard high above his head. When they were entering our half of the debatable country some fool started to fire, setting off a dozen others to pull their triggers.

The Turks turned about and made for home at a shambling trot. Then the fire died again and the peacemakers steadied their retreat. When Bargi called out once more to reassure the runners, they came back reluctantly, the standard-bearer holding his flag at top height. They drew quite near, near enough for me to see clearly their appearance.

The standard-bearer was a cut-throat looking fellow with a black moustache and a dark complexion. He was dressed in a green uniform and had one of those strange pleated caps on his head. Throughout all the dealings he spoke no word.

The man beside him, the empty-handed man, was dressed as an officer and proved to be a doctor. He was a man of manners — a gentleman. He came to the parley with French on his lips. The two men crossed the half-line boundary and came so close in that the colonel put up his hand to stop them, lest they arrive on top of our works.

"Tell them to stay there, Bargi," the colonel broke out. "Tell them to come no further!" Bargi halted them. He had taken courage; he spoke fluently and seemed to enjoy his importance. His face glowed with satisfaction and sweat.

"Get up, Bargi," the colonel said of a sudden. "Go out and meet them. It's quite safe, man. Go on!"

Poor little Bargi collapsed. It was one matter to peep over a parapet top, but quite another to stand up in the open like a tree, being a target for all the world. He gave the colonel a look of agony.

"Hurry up, man!" was all he got for his trouble.

He began his climb, but I had to scramble up first and pull him up the rest of the way. He made no attempt to go further, which did not matter, as the Turks had arrived within talking distance.

Yet it seemed fate would refuse us our parley, for someone let a machine gun loose — Australian or Turk I do not know. The bullets sang beside my head like a swarm of mad bees. This was no time for: "After you, sir." Bargi tumbled back into the trench, and I jumped down on top of him.

A brisk burst of rifle fire broke out on both sides, and then died all of a sudden. Next I was up on the parapet again. The Turkish peacemakers had run for their own lines, but now they returned.

Bargi was disinclined to make a second appearance in the open, but presently he stood on top beside me. The Turks were near at hand again, too close for the

211

colonel's pleasure. He waved Bargi forward in abrupt fashion. With great reluctance Bargi advanced.

Their meeting was like a congress of dancing masters. They put their hands to their foreheads and bowed profoundly. They advanced and bowed once more. They smiled with utmost courtesy and bowed anew.

Next they fell to talking loudly, but in the accents of men who ask the others' good health and who rejoice at the fineness of the day. And while they talked I picked out a seat on the mound before the parapet and sat down to watch.

Two great armies, the Turkish army and the troops of Australasia, were jamming the mouths of the trenches and staring one another in the face. Men who had lived days on end between two narrow, sunbaked walls, men who had lifted heads above a certain level at risk of their lives, now looked over the great bare country and filled their lungs with breezes from the sea.

Clear white clouds floated in the sky, sowing the ground with shadows. There were earthy reds, greens and blues and greys splashed over the picture. There were glistening patches of sand, and in the background were the Turkish hills leaning against the sky.

And rank after rank, from foot to skyline, stood soldiers in their thousands. The reserves were countless. To the right and to the left were our men, their heads lifted over the parapets or sitting on top of the trenches, swinging their legs. And between the armies lay the disputed land, pock-marked with dead men and broken rifles.

212

Where I sat the ground fell sharply away. A few yards down the slope rested three of our dead comrades, lying with heads close together. And wherever you looked you would see parts of bodies — a hand, an elbow, a pair of boots protruding from a mound, or the flutter of a piece of coat. Burials had taken place by night and graves had been dug in great haste in the hard, stony ground. The mounds over the graves had settled and betrayed their secrets.

Of Turks fallen in the last attack there was no end; it was a day's task to count them.

Word came down the line that General Runner was parleying with the enemy. I looked across, but all I could see was several men standing together.

As soon as the fire of both armies hushed, a number of Turks jumped from their trenches and snatched up rifles, which lay in scores about the field. Hastily men staggered home loaded to their limits with their booty.

The colonel let out a bellow. "Stop those men! Stop them this minute! Bargi, stop those men!"

Bargi grasped what was wanted and pointed it out to the flagbearers. With lusty shouting the men were recalled, but by that time the enemy had gained more than fifty rifles.

It was our last interruption. It seemed the enemy asked a truce for the burial of their dead. Bargi ran forwards and backwards, swollen with importance.

The colonel could do no more than receive the message, but the brigadier, who was with the other group, had more power. In due time word arrived empowering the colonel to announce that, next

213

morning, the enemy may send a staff officer by way of Gaba Tepe, where the matter would be discussed.

Bargi floundered over the explanation, and a lieutenant of infantry climbed up to help him. The man must have been among the largest in the army. "You'll be a good advertisement for Australia," the colonel said.

Seeing I wished to go too, he added, "No, Lake, this is not your stunt."

It was all over presently. The men of truce agreed to take back the message. Firing would open again in a few minutes.

Once more the Turks saluted, once more they bowed to us and each other. Our men came this way and the enemy turned the other way.

The colonel gathered up glasses and periscope and we went off to tea. On the way we ran into a party placing a trench mortar in position. Further along we met men hurrying up with ammunition. We had roared at Turkish treachery, but who shall say our honour was shining bright?

As I sat at tea, firing broke out again all around us.

As arranged, a Turkish staff officer rode into our lines the following day. A short time later he rode away again.[37] The next morning he reappeared, and this time they seemed to have come to an agreement. It was arranged that there would be a nine-hour truce.[38] Certain rules had been established. Parties of limited numbers from both sides would be allowed over so many yards and neither party might penetrate beyond

214

halfway. We would take their dead to them and they would bring our dead to us.

The day and the hour came round — peace fell over both armies. Such silence was very strange. About the middle of the morning the colonel set off as usual for the trenches and we started the rounds as on any other day at the B Battery observing station. Not a shot was to be heard and the trenches were emptier of men than I had ever seen them.

Without delay we arrived at C Battery on The Pimple, where we joined Colonel Monash, Major Andrews and Major White. Behind C Battery and before A, the five of us climbed from the trenches onto open ground. Though the sun was out the day was cool, and it was pleasant to stand at ease in the open. A great gathering had come about on No-Man's-Land. It was like a day at the races with a shabby crowd in attendance.

The rule limiting the number of parties was slackly enforced and anyone tying a white bandage to his arm to denote stretcher-bearer could go where he wanted. In this way many were exploring on their own account. Some exchanged mementoes with the enemy and saw what was to be seen. The camera fiend was at large.

The burial of the dead went forward in harmony, if not in love. Our fellows were good-willed enough and eager with curiosity, but among the enemy were many glum countenances, for it is but chilly amusement gazing into the faces of your own dead. There were many strange sights to be found within a few hundred yards. At one place was a crater in the ground where a shell had burst; round it lay eight dead men, like chickens come to feed at a basin. It was the prettiest bit of shooting that you might wish to see.

And not so very far away was a gully, maybe twenty yards long, half that wide and half again that deep. Turkish stretcher-bearers gathered dead from everywhere and tumbled them here. The place became choked with hundreds of bodies, lying a dozen deep. They made me catch my breath. But it was when we turned to go over to A Battery that we passed the scene it will take me longest to forget.

Four of our own fellows lay on their backs in the grass, all within a few paces. They were men who had fallen in the first rush up from Anzac Cove and had been overlooked. Their clothes were unstained, for no rains had touched them, and their hats were still cocked to one side in the jauntiest manner.

The first man was a skeleton, his bones picked clean by birds and foxes. His skull looked out between the tunic and the hat, and through the small bones of his hands fine grasses had woven a mat.

Fierce suns had done otherwise with the next man. He was lying on his back and his flesh had decayed under the skin, which had turned into dark parchment, drawn tightly over the bones. Every hair on his head and hands had remained. Face and hands were as tiny as those of a child, yet his face was full of expression, and terrible to look upon. The third man was similar to the second.

216

The fourth man had swollen up and afterwards sunk down again. His flesh was so spongy you could knock pieces out of him with a walking stick.

And those four men had been filled with great foolish hopes but a few weeks before. Amen! Amen!

CHAPTER
TWELVE

THE SINKING OF HMS *TRIUMPH*

The weeks marched by, one upon the heels of the next. The summer heat arrived and all day long the sun stared at the baked ground and the flies multiplied beyond imagination. The enemy, sitting in the opposite trenches, was less terrible than this pitiless heat. There was no savour in our food and our water ration was far too small to quench our thirsts.

One wit suggested that the best way to kill the Turks would be to lob over tins of bully beef and hardtack biscuits into their lines and deny them water.

We were no further forward than the day we had landed, which seemed an eternity ago. Typhoid and dysentery began to stalk abroad.

Between the attacks, the fellows sat or lay all day long in a sort of dog's doze.

Many put up awnings of waterproof sheets or blankets over their dugouts, but the heat below was close and sickly. Fellows were bare-legged and stripped naked to the waist. Some had big patches of broken skin where the sun had blistered them raw, and others were burnt brown like walnuts.

Groups of men smoked, wrote letters or talked. There was little said about the war, which had long since failed to interest them. What the men enjoyed were everlasting stories of racehorses and prize fights and endless boasts about girls. And many liars told and retold their most brilliant lies in the long fiery hours between the rise and the set of the sun.

As summer wore on and the fighting slackened away to skirmishes, there came much talk of reinforcements of men and guns and a second attempt to take the Gallipoli Peninsula by storm. There was much talk, but nothing happened. No reinforcements arrived.

Endless suns baked the earth to brick and parched the seeds of hope in the men's hearts. The stretcher-bearers took their loads down to the beach, and it was a trench won here and a trench lost there — that was all. One looked in vain for transport ships entering the cove.[39]

Colonel Jackson was a man of habit. We tramped uphill and downhill in the morning and in the evening. We had our battle and fired off our allotted rounds with energy. The sun peeled the skin from the end of the colonel's nose and burned his face a fierce red. His clothes began to wear out, so he changed them for a private's issue; as a consequence, a great deal of his glory departed. But his keenness stayed undimmed.

Our targets changed little. The enemy might bring up a new battery to replace an old one. Steadily the Turks strengthened their trenches and dug them towards ours — we did the same towards theirs.

The Turks made a fortress on a particular hill. From our side the hill was no more than a sandbagged mound with a small bullet-blasted sapling standing up at one point. The sapling was not outstanding, but in that otherwise barren country it made a landmark. It was strange that the enemy allowed it to stay. Colonel Jackson pointed it out to a friend. "They're doing an awful lot of work over there," he said. "You see where I mean, that mound with the stick on it. It reminds you of that book or song — what's its name, 'The Trail of the Lonesome Pine' or something." With these words the colonel had christened the hill "Lonesome Pine".

The enemy made a second fortress on another hill, which became known as Jackson's [Johnston's] Jolly. The colonel wagged his head and was full of misgiving. The Jolly was named after him on account of his fears of it.

There would be days when the sun was less terrible, and sea and sky were calm with the wonderful blue of the Mediterranean. Then the open country between us and Achi Baba became a forbidden Eden, covered with sunshine. I forget how often the colonel and I stared at it. "Look at it, look at it," he would mutter. "What a place for love and fishing!"

Towards evening the D Battalion officers congregated at the top of Shrapnel Valley in a curtained dugout they used as an office. They drifted there in ones and twos to smoke and yawn and stare at the sea.

From there you looked down the length of Shrapnel Valley on a straggle of untidy tents, sandbagged dugouts and tin sheds.

220

The signallers wagged to one another to keep in practice and the reinforcements drilled on a flat open space at the lower end. A few shells might be travelling forwards and backwards, but frequently there was no more sound than the lazy crack of the snipers.

Overlooking this, the D Battalion officers sat on up-ended packing cases and smoked. They always had the beautiful blue sky overhead and the beautiful blue sea to look at.

One late afternoon the colonel sat with them, and not far off I leaned against the bank, exchanging news with the telephonists in the office. "Who would think this was war?" said the colonel, rubbing his nose with the end of the periscope.

Without responding to that rhetorical question one of the officers said, "You had a gun blown out yesterday, didn't you?"

"Yes. I think it can be fixed up," replied the colonel. "Three men went with it."

And then he nodded his head with great sadness. "You can get new guns; but you can't send down to Hell for new gunners."

After a pause the colonel continued. "Did you read what General Ian Hamilton said in brigade orders? 'The incomparable Twenty-ninth!' You can't easily beat 'incomparable'. I suppose when a general hasn't had his name in the paper for a few weeks, he starts writing 'incomparable' and 'glorious' and 'magnificent' to describe his troops; and then the people at home say, 'Those poor men have been through a hard time. That general must be a hell of a clever fellow.'"

221

During those weeks one might look down Shrapnel Valley and not realise we were at war. There were no longer uniformed men about. Many men wore flannel shirts open at the neck and trousers or knickerbockers cut above the knee and legs bare the rest of the way — little remained of their original uniform.

Roads worn solid by the passage of many feet led to the principal places, and the thick scrub that once had made this valley so difficult and so romantic had long ago gone as firewood for the cooks. I have seen mining camps with the same appearance.

But then it became apparent again that we were at war, as the enemy sent us half a dozen big shells at tea-time and on the way up or down you passed a stretcher-bearer making the journey to the beach.

Once I stumbled upon a dead man lying on the side of the road. His lower body was naked and mottled and his two legs stuck stiffly into the air with toes apart. Although I saw nobody attending to him, he had vanished by the time I came back.

Another day there came a great burst of clapping from the lower part of the valley, so that fellows left their work and turned about to know what had happened. Presently news hurried along that the war was over as the Kaiser had murdered the Crown Prince. Later I heard that the applause was because a well-known shirker or "dugout king" had been tempted from his funk-hole on that peaceful morning.

We met a little man one tea-time just below Infantry Headquarters. We came down from our evening battle and he was striding up.

"Good day, sir," he said and saluted.

"Hullo, captain," shouted the colonel. "Thought you were down at Helles?"

"Back again," said the captain.

"You had a hot time down there, didn't you?"

"Pretty hot," replied the captain. "Their machine guns played the very deuce. Did you know two or three men with machine guns can hold up a battalion? Before very long war will be one man in an armoured box, turning a treadle and setting fifty machine guns going!"

"Well so long, captain, I'm off to tea." And away we went.

The monotony of each and every day put men at their wits' end to escape the place. Fellows went sick unaccountably, and had strange bullet wounds in hand or foot in an attempt to get sent home.

This brings to mind a man I met near Clayton's trenches. The enemy was giving us hurry-up with five- and six-inch shells, which arrived onc or two per minute and burst with a dull roar. Some fell ahead of us and some behind, and there was no reason why one should not fall atop of us. Therefore, as we had no call here, it was prudent to choose a healthier location.

At a traverse corner a parapet had come down and a man stood trapped by the legs, pulling to and fro to get free. Sitting on my knees I dragged the dirt away. Soon I had loosened him so that his own efforts could do the rest. He came free, panting and rather scared, but unhurt. I jumped up again and the colonel, who waited nearby, set the pace anew.

I had forgotten all about the man by tea-time, when I met a procession going down to the beach. The centre figure was the hero of the afternoon, hobbling along with a man supporting him on either side. A third man carried his equipment and a fourth his pack and blankets. "Off for a holiday," thought I. "Well, there's luck."

The British battleship HMS *Triumph*, which had laboured long and hard in our cause, was torpedoed by a German submarine in sight of the army. We came out of the trenches upon a group of officers and men staring to sea with glasses to their eyes. The men were tongue-tied, except for one or two murmurs of regret.

The battleship lay not far off from the great gun of Gaba Tepe and was listing to one side. Destroyers raced to her aid from all over the bay. They closed in about her and began the work of rescue.

The commander of Gaba Tepe seized the opportunity of a lifetime and opened fiercely with shrapnel. The destroyers blazed back, the flashes winking like Morse lights. Although a brisk engagement followed, the work of rescue went forward. Presently the *Triumph* heeled over completely and disappeared, except for her red keel, which kept floating for some time. The destroyers remained to pick up survivors and next they dispersed. Then the gun of Gaba Tepe fell silent.

We, who were watching from the hilltop, put away our glasses and looked at one another. There was a great muttering and shaking of heads. "Damned bad. Damned bad!"

This was the first warning that German submarines had come so far abroad. The navy took fright and steamed away. Soon there remained only destroyers and other light craft. Submarine scares followed and hunts were organised, with aeroplanes patrolling the bay and destroyers following.

The aeroplanes of both armies grew bold, and our men sailed over the enemy trenches to observe and throw bombs. The enemy treated us similarly, usually at tea-time. Occasionally Yards, the adjutant, went up in a plane. The colonel would crane his neck and watch him, saying, "I shall not try to fly until I become an angel. I'm too nervous to go up into the air."

German planes circled overhead in a fashion most annoying to those below. When a bomb came free, it gave no hint of its target. Then came the final rush, a moment of fierce suspense, followed by the roar of the bursting bomb, the screams of the wounded and dying, and the cry for stretcher-bearers.

Compared with the infantry, we were relatively safe. Nevertheless Death's fingers touched us as well. First Ned Thompson had been killed, followed by my good old friend Bill Eaves. And then poor Lieutenant Lewis's turn had come.

I had finished breakfast half an hour ago and now loafed near my dugout while the colonel shaved himself. A corporal came over to me, dirty and very tired. He looked at me, head to one side, until I wondered what he wanted. At last he said: "Heard about poor Lewis?"

"What about Lewis?" I answered, remembering the young lieutenant with the baby face who was planning to get married when he came home.

"Had his head blown off this morning."

"My God!" I said. We looked at each other a little while. "Damned bad luck for poor Lewis."

And after that, what more was there to say? The corporal shrugged his shoulders, lingered a moment and went off to his dugout. I sat down on the ground to wait for the colonel.

It was early yet, but already the sun menaced us. Flies in their tens of thousands blackened every shady place and made ready to drowse and drone through the noon. I brushed them from my lips for the thousandth time since breakfast. While sitting there with my head drooping I thought a little of Lewis and a lot of nothing at all. Sands climbed down the path towards me and I got up.

"Lake, the colonel won't want you this morning. You are to wait here for Bombardier Norris and a couple of stretcher-bearers to guide them to Lewis. You know where Lewis is — in the communication trench leading to Clayton's. Afterwards you can go on to the B Battery observing station. The colonel is going that way."

I answered, "Yes, sir."

Sands said nothing more, yet he did not go away and stayed on, smiling vacantly and looking at his fingers.

After a while I said: "There won't be any of the first lot left by the time this is over. We joined up too soon."

He replied with a snorting laugh. "Yes, at this rate it will be the 100th Battalion which returns to Melbourne in triumph, not the First or the Second. And the girls will hooray and the papers will talk about heroes and it will be forgotten that we ever went."

The lieutenant waved the flies from his face and then continued: "Well, you must do something about poor Lewis." And away he went.

I sat down again and dozed as before in the sweltering heat. Norris did not turn up for a long while. Finally, between ten and eleven he and the two stretcher-bearers came climbing up the hill. The sun was high up and the air blistering with heat. The stretcher party dropped onto the ground, panting and perspiring. We lit cigarettes, smoked for a while and talked wearily, exchanging news. At the finish of the cigarettes I said: "How about it now?"

"Right-oh." The bearers picked up their stretcher and we started to climb the hill.

We passed Infantry Headquarters and up the next pinch to the mouth of the communication trench where Lewis was said to be. The place was quite deserted, except for hosts of flies. The trench was high and narrow, with many turns and safe enough from shrapnel. We tramped along, panting and perspiring. Presently we saw the body of Lewis, lying on his back and largely covered with sacks. He looked no different from a sleeping man, for most people covered themselves in this way for shade and to escape the flies.

But the trench walls told the story, as for a dozen yards the brains of Lewis clung to them. They could be traced by the flies that had settled on them. On the trench floor were pieces of scalp and bits of raw flesh — a most sickening sight.

We said nothing, brushed the flies from our faces and somebody put down the stretcher. Out came cigarettes. The heat and the steepness of the slope forced a rest before we started work. The stretcher-bearers sat on the stretcher. I settled opposite, and Norris crouched at the head of the body. The flies, which had been disturbed by our coming, settled again at their task. As there was no breeze the blue smoke of our cigarettes curled straight into the air. The flies camped in black masses on the sacking that lay over the corpse, boots and leggings poked from underneath the cover. They were big boots — Lewis was a tall fellow and his feet had not been the least part of him.

We were at the straightest part of the trench, which ran a dozen yards without a turning. Because of that the fatal shell had found its way in. It was one chance in a hundred, but the ballot had been against Lewis. He had gone and we had stayed behind to sweat and curse the flies.

There was a shovel near us. I got up and collected pieces of his head, put them near his body and covered them over with the sacking. I took care not to explore underneath the sack, for I had no relish for what would be revealed.

So this was the end of Lewis, the beloved of his family, the fellow with the face of a girl. His blond hair was now clotted with blood and dirt, and the worms would make a bridal chamber of the sockets that had held his blue eyes. Presently there would be tears shed for him when the news went home, but he himself needed no pity. He had done his duty and was off duty till the Angel Gabriel called "Reveille".

When our cigarettes were finished Norris said to the others, "What about it?"

"Right-oh!" And the four of us got to our feet. We spread out the stretcher and laid the body on it without moving the sack. A last search was made for remains that might have escaped us. Then began the long sad journey down to the beach.

Afterwards I went to the B Battery observing station to meet up with the colonel. On my way I noticed that the mail had arrived and saw men sniffing around on the chance of spotting something of their own. Letters were the one interest remaining to our drooping army. A good or bad mail made or marred a fellow's temper for the week. This collection was for the infantry so I passed it by without interest.

CHAPTER
THIRTEEN

PUTTING ON A SHOW FOR THE ENEMY

We had stirred up a hornet's nest and had only ourselves to blame.

The colonel had announced: "If you hit a man right and hit him left and then kick him in the backside, he is generally too surprised to do anything. That's our stunt for this afternoon."

And so we had fixed up this little show.

Our three batteries — two Scottish howitzer batteries and a New Zealand one — agreed to engage the enemy at the same moment. We were to slap at him as soon as he opened his mouth for the afternoon battle. We had extra ammunition to spend. The colonel was like a schoolboy on holidays and invited a couple of infantrymen to join us. We went away to a new observing station connected by telephone with the old place. I sat beside the phone to take messages in case of emergency.

The battle opened well for us. The Turkish guns only sniped at us, and very soon we shut them up altogether. The colonel peered into his periscope and chuckled.

Then all of a sudden the Turks woke up and answered with a volley of big shells along our first line of trenches. It was our turn to be surprised. Our

230

laughter lost its hearty ring. Our little party, who had engineered this business, had chosen a safe place for the present. But to the left of us matters looked most uncomfortable and the blameless infantry suffered.

I sat by the colonel's feet. From his brief remarks and the explosions I gathered how matters went. Our own shells were tearing overhead. With lively faces and lively movements the men pushed past us on some duty or other.

The telephonist crouched at my back, receiver strapped to his head. He repeated the colonel's orders in monotonous voice and called out the replies.

Being the sleeping partner in the fight I crossed my legs, put my chin in the cup of my hand and waited for what might happen. The colonel's face was crimson from the sun and from his feelings. Clearly something was going wrong, for he was losing patience. He shifted from one leg to the other and frowned while staring through the periscope. He snapped out orders at the telephonist.

"Why have the New Zealanders shut up shop?" the colonel burst out. "What's happened to them? Find out from Sands what's happened to them."

The telephonist buzzed but got no answer. He buzzed again, with like result. For the next few minutes he buzzed and called in turn. Then he said: "Can't raise them, sir." The colonel was too busy to hear and he went on calling.

"Have you got that through?" said the colonel, all of a sudden.

"No, sir. Can't raise them."

"What's up?"

"Don't know, sir. Line must be cut."

"Oh, damn!" The colonel chewed his top lip. "Are you there, Lake?"

"Yes, sir." I got up.

"Run down to Lieutenant Sands and ask what's happened to the New Zealanders. Tell him the line is cut and he must send someone along to mend it at once. Hurry, man, there's no time to lose!"

I knocked the ash from my cigarette and hurried along the trench. I turned to the left and almost at once passed the traverse corner, so the group I had left was out of sight.

I went at a trot wherever the trench was empty, but that was seldom the case. Much of the way the men were wide awake and in most places they stood to arms, with anxiety on their faces. Usually I progressed at a run or a fast walk, but there were times when shells whistled overhead, so I had to get down and elbow my way forward. The fellows talked loudly to one another and those who knew me for an artilleryman called out to know what we were doing up there.

In truth I was advancing into the danger zone. The roar of the bursting shells was more terrible and there were frequent marks of damage. All at once I came on a wrecked machine gun emplacement where a shell had entered. Blood was spilled about aplenty. Two men dug feverishly into the upheaved earth and I saw the legs of a buried body sticking out. A dead man lay face down in the trench. He was covered with earth, and his eyes and mouth were filled up with it. I pushed past them.

One of the diggers called after me: "The parapet's down there, mate. Look slick as you pass the open bit. The snipers are watching it for their next hit."

I waved a hand to show I had heard and dodged by the open part — sure enough, two bullets chipped the earth behind me. Our trenches here were deep and safe enough to withstand small stuff. But these big howitzer shells were a different matter and nothing was proof against them.

I puffed at the end of my cigarette, for it was the last of the week's issue. It tasted cheap and nasty. When half the journey was done, I heard the scream of a shell right overhead. There was a thud and then a dull roar, which made my ears sing. The ground started trembling and the parapet a few yards away crashed in. A body was thrown face up at my very feet.

There came another scream hard on the first, another thud, another roar, making my head buzz with the noise. The parapet beside me toppled down and the earth flooded up, trapping me round the ankles. The ground shook to its centre and I swear the dead man clapped his hands.

I tried to keep my head cool and kicked myself free, jumped over the dead man and clambered across the mount of earth that threatened to swamp me.

Just then there was a noise of footsteps and three men with white, twitching faces ran up as though the devil was at their heels. The sight of them pulled me together. I put my arms on either side of the trench and faced them coldly. The leading man was forced to come to a standstill. I said a few things to them, and from the way I spoke they must have taken me for an officer. Within seconds I had them scuttling back to their posts like the cowards they were.

I ran on again until I found my destination. Lieutenant Sands was leaning out of his funk-hole in a bored manner.

"Message, sir, from the CO," I called out. "Find out why New Zealand battery has ceased fire."

A look of sadness crossed Sands's face. "Lake," he said, "you're too slow to arrive in time for your own bloody funeral. I got that message two minutes ago over the phone from Brigade HQ."

I sat down to get my breath back. The butt of the cigarette was in my lips and I spat it out. The whole affair had taken place in the smoking of half a cigarette.

Summer wore on and came to its height. All day long the sun stared from a cloudless sky onto baked earth. The midday heat was so fierce that even the flies died. Dysentery and typhoid took hold in earnest. The hours were so many, it seemed the day would never end — the days were so many, it seemed the summer would last forever. Men woke in the morning with the languor of despair. Instead of fighting, the colonel vanished to the dugout of a friend and left me to stare over the desolate No-Man's-Land to watch for the flash of guns.

A keen haze shivered above the empty space until the sun touched the horizon in the form of a crimson ball. The nights were kinder than the days, as at sunset an evening breeze moved from the sea. So one could gather energy for the morrow.

Often I sat in front of my dugout staring at the setting sun. The sky faded, the sea grew dim and shadowy and overhead stars came out. The cool of night moved abroad. The valley grew hushed. Then shells scattered in the sky when a burst of rapid fire broke from the trenches. Sometimes our guns opened their mouths and sent shells moving through the dark like red-hot cinders. But more often, a hush fell on the valley.

Most nights some of the fellows came over for a visit. It was the hour when men sucked at their pipes and opened their hearts. Many a strange love story was told under the eyes of the waiting stars. You saw the red glow of cigarettes and pipes and a face lit up for a moment. And after the stories were told, as silently as they arrived, the men went off to their cramped dugouts. It remained for me to unroll blankets and waterproof sheets, to undress and lie down and forget care in sleep.

In the course of time the enemy received considerable reinforcements of guns and ammunition and while the newspapers were declaring Turkey was on the verge of collapse, our trenches and sandbags were knocked on top of us.

One evening Sands wandered over at sunset to squat down by my dugout. He had done this several times before — the habit was growing on him. Maybe melancholy had overcome even his imperturbable

235

spirit. We sat side by side staring at the sun. That evening my visitor was strangely depressed.

"Lake," he said, "what do you think of it all? Will we get out in one piece?"

I shrugged my shoulders. When Sands got no answer he laughed ironically.

Below us a great many fellows were going down to the sea with towels about their necks and I wanted to join them. But Sands sat where he was and as the senior officer I must wait for him to make a move.

At last I responded to his question. "The odds are we will be shot with six- or eight-inch shells. There ought to be a rule: nothing bigger than three-inch allowed."

Sands chuckled.

I continued with feeling: "A fellow's not safe anywhere — it's hard on a fellow's nerves waiting for the bullet that'll blow him apart . . . I know you have a bad time every night where you are. It's the worst place in the line."

"Yes," Sands replied, "it's pretty unhealthy there about five o'clock. They've got our range properly. This evening the Turks started to lob six-inch shells beside me. I thought I would see how many I could stand. I waited for three and then left. The next one came into the observing station and blew the place to blazes. Lucky I shifted." He gave another of those ironic laughs.

Soon afterwards he went away.

I picked up a towel and joined the throng moving to the beach. Half the army bathed at sundown. At that time the beach was filled with naked men treading over the treacherous pebbles to the sea, while others were drying and dressing themselves. The piers overflowed with divers and the waves were dotted with the heads of swimmers and there was more laughter and shouting than during the whole rest of the day. But a false note jarred this seaside harmony. Day and night Beachy Bill, the gun the Germans had donated to the Turks, waited with devilish patience. There would come a whistle, a bang and a great spluttering on the waves or woodwork of the piers. Those diving from the jetties raced for cover and swimmers struck out for land. Beneath the cliffs men looked into each other's eyes and laughed nervously. And maybe the cry for stretcher-bearers arose.

After their swim the men would line up to fill their water bottles for the next day.

One morning at breakfast time a man gathering firewood climbed too high up the opposite hill. We watched him, realising he took a great risk. And indeed, a sniper's bullet hit him through the chest. He rolled down the hill and screamed like a wounded hare — never had I heard a man scream like that before. After rolling a short distance he became tangled up in a tree root. Then stretcher-bearers arrived and took charge. I don't know what became of him, but my appetite for breakfast was ruined.

Another time I sat at sunset in my dugout yarning with one of the fellows. The enemy was shelling us in a happy-go-lucky way when a piece of casing from a high-explosive shell whizzed past and grazed me on the side of my head. I came off with a headache and a little blood drawn, but it was a close touch.

CHAPTER
FOURTEEN

WHAT BRAVE HOPES, WHAT COURAGE SPENT

We seemed to come no nearer to victory as summer wore on. News from the battlefields of France was depressing. It was the time of the Russian retreat. Wisely, we were given good and bad news impartially, which made us believe the good news when it arrived. Uncensored telegrams from the Reuter's News Bureau were posted daily on biscuit boxes by the beach and on notice boards at the various headquarters. Men coming down to the beach to fill their water bottles or to bathe crowded around the announcements. When the reading was over the men cursed the heat, the flies, the monotony and their misfortune. Then they tramped uphill again.

The old fierceness had left the enemy as it had us. Men who had been strong and healthy were now gaunt, their faces lined and cheeks sunken.[40] At long intervals one or other goaded himself into wrath, but more generally all there was to be heard was the crack of snipers' bullets and the occasional voice of a gun.

Then there were more rumours of reinforcements and a fresh advance. Ammunition and guns appeared on the beach. Batteries of five-inch and six-inch howitzers arrived and with them came bargeloads of shells. Provision depots were converted into sheltered places in anticipation of the reinforcements. A gleam of hope lit the future.

The colonel spoke to me one day as we passed the fork where Shrapnel and Monash Valleys join. "You've done your turn, Lake. I can send you down to the column as acting bombardier."

"Sir," I replied, "acting bombardier is a thankless job. The men know an acting bombardier draws no extra pay and they value him accordingly."

"Well, a man has to make a beginning somewhere."

Next day I was ordered down to the column not as acting, but as a full bombardier.

Our column had dug themselves into the ruins of our former Brigade Headquarters. They were handy to the beach and had an uninterrupted view of the sea. The place had much to recommend it, but it suffered from the attentions of Beachy Bill and his comrade from Anafarta. As a newcomer I had poor choice of dugouts, but I picked one in a hollow, screened from Beachy Bill and moderately protected from the large Anafarta gun. Here I laid out my kit and awaited what might be in store.

Soon after my promotion to bombardier I became seriously ill. For several weeks I had suffered from dysentery, but that was common among us.[41] Now a terrible weariness took hold of me, with a splitting headache and painful cramps in my intestines. I thought the attack would soon be over but it got no better. I wondered what was becoming of me.

I had no complaint to lodge on the score of duty. Two days after arrival I was detailed three men and sent a little way up the valley to guard a provision depot. Reinforcements now were expected daily. I divided the guard into shifts of two hours on duty and four hours off. After seeing that the work was carried out, I could call my time my own.

I put up an awning and slept under its shadow through the heat of the day.

About five o'clock in the afternoon the enemy put in a few rounds of some ancient field piece, half cannon and half trench mortar. It hurled a rough iron ball up into the air, which shattered into three or four pieces. The provision stack seemed to be the target. In addition, visiting German planes habitually left a calling card in the shape of a bomb.

Around six o'clock I started towards the beach and took with me water bottles that needed filling. By that time the first of the bathers were coming down and most of them carried empty water bottles slung over their shoulders.

Below the junction of Monash and Shrapnel Valleys began a wide deeply cut road, built by the sappers in the days after we landed. On the left was a large, roughly fenced cemetery full of well-maintained graves. As afternoon declined, this sheltered road became crowded with pedestrians. At the end of twenty or thirty yards it emptied onto a hillock overlooking the sea, with a square of ground quite destitute of cover from shellfire. The path ran round it and led down to the beach.

The ocean, always blue and mostly calm, was now emptier than usual. The transports had long since steamed away and enemy submarines had scared the main body of the fleet. Inshore, round about the jetties, there was much more movement. All day barges of provisions and ammunition arrived.

There were also pinnaces taking the wounded out to the hospital ship. The army medical men had a jetty of their own, decorated with a Red Cross flag. At the foot of the road other jetties overflowed with men carrying provisions and ammunition from the barges or pumping out fresh water. At sunset these workers were exchanged for scores of naked bathers.

There was always something of interest on the beach, be it the Reuter's board with its telegrams, a chance of meeting acquaintances, or the sight of other men working while you loafed. Then there was always the dread of being hit by Beachy Bill. You remembered him most acutely while waiting in a long queue of men filling water bottles; water tanks were his favourite targets.

Transports had arrived and there were stacks of provisions larger than houses. There were stores of fodder. There were field hospitals and headquarters of generals, bakers' shops, butchers' shops, cobblers' workshops, post offices and more. From end to end, the beach was crowded with soldiers and mules. At the far end of the beach, better protected from enemy fire, they were building vast ammunition reserves, and guns and their wagons accumulated here for the expected advance.

242

Seldom did I go further than the Australian post office, where I had acquaintances. In the same neighbourhood was a wire enclosure where prisoners of war were kept until they could be shipped away. Those Turks I saw there were shabby, depressed creatures, ill shod and clad. Many had hair and beards streaked with grey. Yet our own appearance could scarcely have been better. The Turkish prisoners had put up some kind of shelter and sat and dozed in it all day and at evening wandered round the enclosure with morose looks.

The shadow of Death over the land did not prevent certain spirits from seeking to turn an honest or dishonest penny. A trade began in eggs, chocolate, tinned fish and cigarettes, smuggled over from the nearby island of Imbros. Profits were as high as 300 to 400 per cent. Eggs at four and five shillings the dozen were sold out at once. I have been down there at four in the morning to get some.

My guard duty at the provision depot continued for the better part of a fortnight, and during that time considerable preparations for our attack were made. Batteries arrived ashore, including a number of howitzers. Some of them were concealed among the gullies running from the sea, others were parked on the beach. Men unloaded so many shells it seemed we never could fire such a number. We had a hard nut to crack, but this time we seemed to have the proper nutcrackers.

Presently the first of the reinforcements appeared on the scene. Those I saw — and I saw thousands — were newly formed battalions showing youthful faces. There were English troops and well-equipped Indian regiments — turbaned Sikhs and Gurkhas — who dug themselves in at all unoccupied places. The valleys and gullies filled up with them. We were quick to experience the change of numbers; henceforward the filling of water bottles and cans was a bitter business, as there was not enough to go round. Three or four days must be spent before the attack and the English had no luck in that time. The big shells, fired haphazardly by the enemy, often found targets in our valleys and severely tried the nerves of the new arrivals.

When the English soldiers arrived, my guard on the stores ended. An officer turned up one evening and took over the place. I was neither glad nor sorry at the change.

I dismissed my men, rolled up my blankets and went back to the armaments column. To tell the truth, ill health had brought me to the end of my tether. My strength was leaving me — it was hard work just to walk uphill and I could not travel far without a rest. In the mornings, I did not know how I should last through the day.

The following night the few remaining men of our group had to drag a battery of heavy guns from the beach into position on our left flank. The work went forward in the dark, with no more than the occasional light of a lantern. We toiled away in long lines, moving the guns by ropes. In quiet places we passed drafts from Indian regiments, from where brief commands and the jangle of arms came to us. When our journey ended, the beach was still busy with men at final preparations.

Batteries of guns moved to this and that position — long lines of men carried ammunition after them.

At last our battery was in position, but it still had to be hidden from aircraft. Greenery was scarce and tough to cut when found. So we might not fall asleep over our duty, at intervals shells were fired at random, bursting with blinding flashes in the sky.

Twelve hours later the attack began and our batteries were heavily engaged. By evening the fury of both armies was terrible. Shells of all weights descended upon us and the fierceness of our replies equalled those of the enemy. The big reserve of shells stacked by the guns threatened exhaustion, and a call came for further supplies.

Some men carried a live eighteen-pounder shell on either shoulder. As you left the A Battery trenches to cross the open space to The Pimple, the country seemed furrowed by a gigantic plough. Dead men gaped at you wherever shadows were least thick.

The fury of the Turkish fire had abated for a while, but it was not a journey one would wish to repeat. The climb up the hills and the weight of the shells stole my strength. Though I fell over half a dozen times on the journey, I managed the return empty-handed. I could reach my funk-hole, but I could do no more than that. The gunfire was still knocking at my ears when I went to sleep.

The sounds heard at night woke me to a morning even more terrible than before. I looked out to the sea and saw the ocean filled with a great fleet. The guns of the battleships bellowed with the voices of olden days. We must succeed this time, I thought.

I had difficulty raising my head. A fever burned within me, and my strength seemed gone. I lay back again among the blankets. Again and again broke out the fierce voices of field guns, and the rifle fire rolled up and down tirelessly. The enemy replied with as much spirit, but the beach bore most of their fury. Even the dugout walls vibrated.

Some strength returned as I lay there, but I continued to feel miserable. Presently I pulled clothes on and made breakfast. I drank a little but could not eat. Then I joined the other fellows and together we watched the battle.

I was not on duty before nightfall so the day was my own. The enemy fire continued with great fury and kept us on the threshold of our dugouts. In the afternoon I went down to the tank to fill my water bottle. Next to the road at the bottom of the hill was a small shed that was used as a mortuary; stretcher-bearers coming from the valley left their burdens there. Most days, you would find three or four blanketed forms there; sometimes the number was greater. That day, as I passed on the way to the beach, sixteen bodies lay there in two rows. A party of men arrived for their burial. On my return the shed had filled again.

Near General Headquarters I saw a strange happening. Four men carried a single man who struggled and shouted — they were finding their work no easy matter. At first I thought fear and continual shelling had sent him mad, but later I discovered that he was merely drunk. The party marched slowly, with many pauses for struggle. They moved in the direction of the cells. It was not a pleasant sight at an hour when every man was needed.

I made inquiries about the battle and heard that the English had attacked and gained a large part of the country round Suvla Bay. Numbers of prisoners were arriving under escort of Indians.

The beach was stacked with stretcher-loads of wounded and many hospital ships waited at sea. After filling my water bottle I returned to the column. The assault continued all day, but abated towards evening.

About sunset the sergeant-major sent for me to report at Brigade Headquarters. I made tea, and then rolled together blankets and kit and prepared for the journey. With so little strength left I had difficulty lifting the bundle to my shoulder. I began my journey by the light of the stars.

By this time a great stillness had fallen over the land. The artillery of both sides had shut their mouths. The rifle fire still rolled from end to end of the trenches; but the sound was so even and my ears so used to it that I scarcely heard it. I climbed along the hillside as far as the cutting, which joins Shrapnel Valley with the beach.

The cutting took me to the valley foot. Where the two valleys join I sat down for a rest. There was a cross at the back of me, marking a grave much grown over with scrub. It was the grave of a B Battery corporal I had known well. I found myself wishing we could change places. It seemed impossible to climb the rest of the way up the hill.

The valley was very empty, which may have accounted in part for its stillness. The majority of the English troops had been taken away for the attack on Suvla Bay. Those of our own infantry who were not in the trenches lay low in the hills on either side of the valley, no doubt mistrustful of a second bombardment.

I saw the gleam of a few fires and heard voices.

Eventually I got to my feet and continued along the empty valley, meeting only a mule wagon on the way. Two star shells burst in the sky and a volley of rapid fire broke from the trenches. When the enemy fire died again to an even roll I rested a second time at the foot of the hill where headquarters was dug in. Then I began to climb the last bitter slope. I thought it impossible to reach the top, but I scrambled there at last.

Before reporting to the sergeant-major, I sat down to catch my breath.

Round about me the men sat at the mouths of their funk-holes, talking together and smoking and dreaming. The colonel, with a couple of other men, was in the officers' dugout. He spoke down the phone, relating the day's events.

I looked for the sergeant-major and found him in his dugout, lying on his blankets. He looked tired and ill. A candle in a cigarette tin lit the place. I lowered my head — the roof was low — and peered inside.

"I've come to report for duty, sergeant-major."

He looked at me over the candle and blinked his eyes. I was in shadow and it took him a moment to recognise me.

"Oh, it's you, Lake. You'll be wanted in the morning for observation duty. Brought your kit?"

"Yes, sir," I said and added, "Good night" before going once again to the latrines and then across to the field telephone office.

There I found Wilkinson reading *The Bulletin* by the light of a lantern, receiver by his side. He seemed pleased to see me but said all of a sudden, "You look crook."

"I feel pretty crook," I answered. Then I sat down and asked for the news. Wilkinson had plenty.

"They took Lone Pine," he exclaimed.[42]

"By Jove!" I said. "What about the Jolly?"

"They've not got that yet. They found tons of ammunition in the Lone Pine trenches and there's a report through that our fellows and the Gurkhas have taken Hill 971. It sounds dinkum."

"I think I'll turn in," I said in the end.

He gave me a long look and nodded goodnight.

I went outside to look for an empty dugout and ran into Woods, who suggested I should sleep in his funk-hole. I spread out my blankets and lay down, hoping I might not wake again.

"Take this stretcher case," said the man on the jetty to the man on the barge. My stretcher was lifted up again. I was laid down among the wounded and the dying.

With some effort I opened my eyes and saw that I was lying between two wounded Indian soldiers. The one on the right was motionless and had the pallor of approaching death; the other sat cross-legged and bent

249

over me when he noticed that my eyes were open. In an attempt to make me more comfortable he pulled out the blanket beneath my head so that I might rest easier.

All over the deck of the barge lay bodies of broken men. Drawn faces with shut eyes were turned up to the sky. The deck was filthy, littered with loose straw and manure, as the barge had been claimed in a hurry for this new use.

Then came the bustle of casting off. The pinnace that would tow us to the hospital ship tugged at her cables. When we moved away from the shore I closed my eyes again. The afternoon sun was beating on my face, but a breeze from the ocean spoiled its fury.

The cries from the shore slowly died away, though I still heard the rattle of guns. It had come over the waters to meet me four months before; it came over after me as I floated away.

The barge moved on the calm seas with easy lulling motion. I wanted to sleep but felt I must open my eyes again to see the last of Anzac Cove. As the barge drew away I saw it all: the narrow pebbled beach, the tall bare hills pockmarked with dugouts, the almost vertical cliffs, ravines and gullies. It was an unforgettable picture painted in tones of brown and smoky grey.

What brave hopes lay buried at Anzac Cove, what courage spent, what rich blood spilled. I closed my eyes, and Beachy Bill fired a final salute.

When I opened my eyes again the barge was at a standstill and there were raised voices around me. We were under the shadow of the hospital ship.

250

Once more I heard the rattling of chains as the stretchers were placed in a cradle and lifted aboard by crane. Presently I mounted through the air on my stretcher. Arms came out to steady me and draw me in. And then, for the first time in months, I found myself looking into a woman's face.

EPILOGUE

THE STRAITS IMPREGNABLE, ITS AFTERMATH, AND SYDNEY LOCH, THE "SCARLET PIMPERNEL" OF WORLD WAR II

He had a sense of humour, a sharp eye for character and incident and the knack for reproducing scraps of conversation. His account is both realistic and entertaining . . . the book has a literary as well as historical value.

> H. M. GREEN, *A HISTORY OF AUSTRALIAN LITERATURE*, VOL. 1, 1962, p. 660, DESCRIBING SYDNEY AS A WRITER AND *THE STRAITS IMPREGNABLE*

Semi-comatose because of typhoid fever, with a soaring temperature and a bandage around his head, Sydney withstood a nightmare five-day journey to Alexandria. His stretcher was placed on deck as the bunks in the wards down below were filled with casualties from Lone Pine and Suvla Bay.

Patients suffering from severe dysentery and typhoid fever had to make do with a single bedpan passed from stretcher to stretcher, or use the scuppers as latrines.

Men still capable of walking brought mess tins of food from the canteen to those such as Sydney, who were too weak to stand or walk to get their own. A shortage of doctors and the need for emergency amputations on those with gangrenous wounds meant that little time could be spared for typhoid sufferers.

By 13 August, when the ship reached Alexandria, Sydney was dangerously ill.[1] At No. 17 General Hospital he spent six days on the danger list. He had developed a severe case of polyneuritis, a painful inflammation of the myelin nerve sheath; this was a side effect of the delay in treating his typhoid fever. He spent the next four months in hospital with painfully swollen legs. On 13 December 1915 he was well enough to be transferred to an "enteric convalescent camp" at Port Said.

A Christmas card from his mother brought little comfort. The lease on Harker Lodge had expired, so his parents and Laura had moved to Edensteads, a smaller rented home. His mother, once so active, was now an invalid due to heart problems. Laura was caring for her.

Sydney received three other cards: one from his brother Eric, now promoted to captain and fighting in the trenches in France; another from his brother Charlie, who was working as a mining engineer in central Queensland; and the third from Elsie Blair, the girl who had befriended him during those early days on Kirndean Station. Elsie wrote that her father had died of a heart attack and that she herself was suffering from palpitations. To be nearer to medical care she had moved from the bush to Melbourne.[2]

253

On 3 January 1916, still suffering pain in his swollen legs, Sydney returned to Melbourne on the troop carrier *Ulysses*. A consultant specialist examined his legs and confirmed that he would need crutches for several more months; he also said that if things did not go well, Sydney could be an invalid for life. The one good aspect of his long convalescence was the fact that it gave him a great opportunity to write his war journal.

Like many other Gallipoli veterans in the military hospital, Sydney was plagued with recurring nightmares. In some of them he relived traumatic events such as the agonising death of his friends. Sometimes he would wake up, imagining that shells were screaming overhead and landing beside his bed, then remain awake for the rest of the night. In 1916 hardly anyone had heard of war neurosis (or post-traumatic stress) and there was little treatment for it. Sydney decided that revisiting his past by sorting out his Gallipoli diary would be a "good way of getting events that haunted me out of my mind".

One day Sydney's friend and financial backer of his farm, Arthur le Paturel (Ted in *The Straits Impregnable*), came to visit him in hospital, bringing Sydney's typewriter. He told Sydney he was returning to England to enlist with a cavalry regiment, as he had no wish to join the Anzacs. Then he gave Sydney the bad news that Laura, who was short of funds, wanted to sell the lease of Barwon Banks. Under Old Scottie's management the sheep property had been losing money, so Arthur now agreed with his sister's proposal to sell.

When Sydney protested, Arthur pointed out that in his condition he could scarcely expect to be able to run the grazing property. Someone had shown interest in buying the lease and Sydney's stock, provided they asked realistic prices.

With a shock Sydney realised that after two and a half years of backbreaking work — clearing and fencing the land — all he would receive was the price of his sheep and horses. He also realised that no one would give a semi-cripple a job. The only thing left that might earn him some income was his Gallipoli diary.

On 16 March 1916 Sydney was considered fit enough to return to duty, but due to further complications he was not discharged from hospital until 28 April.

By late February 1916, Sydney had finished typing out his story. By now he was able to walk with the aid of a stick, and one of the first things he did with his new-found independence was take a tram from the hospital to Collins Street and join a private lending library. Elsie Champion, sister of the famous political activist Vida Goldstein and member of the "Women's Peace Army", owned the library. Elsie's husband, portly red-faced Harry Champion, was running a literary agency and editing a magazine called *The Book Lover*. Sydney asked Elsie Champion if her husband would read his manuscript, which he had titled *The Straits Impregnable*. Elsie had trouble persuading her husband to read it: he did not enjoy war diaries and found that very few were sufficiently well written to be publishable.

Harry Champion had become disillusioned by the way the war was going and was distressed by the fact that his favourite nephew had been killed in the trenches. He knew that thousands of young men on each side died in northern France each week, obeying the orders of elderly generals who, in his opinion, were using them as cannon fodder. The public had been misled by the promise that the war would be over quickly and that by Christmas — originally, Christmas 1914! — "our boys" would be home again.

Harry was so incensed by the misinformation that he had written an ironic letter to the Melbourne papers, suggesting that rather than killing off a complete generation of young men, it would be much better to send elderly men like himself to the trenches. The young should be kept alive and allowed to run the war from the safety of headquarters well behind the lines, as the elderly generals were doing. Naturally, the newspapers refused to print what they termed subversive material.

Harry Champion, his wife, Elsie, and her sister, Vida Goldstein, were keen socialists, and wanted a negotiated peace. They posed the question at public meetings why the pompous royal cousin, the Kaiser, and the King of England could not bypass the politicians, come to a peaceful settlement over territorial claims and cease this senseless slaughter of young men on both sides.

It is easy to imagine that Harry Champion picked up Sydney's typed account of his war service without much enthusiasm. However, once he started reading the manuscript he found it gripping . . . he stayed up half the night to finish it. Champion believed that such a truthful account had to be published, as it presented a contrast to the overly romanticised picture of war presented in the local press.

Sydney realised that as a serving soldier, it was unwise to use his own name, so he decided to use "Sydney de Loghe", the name of a Norman ancestor. Harry, acting as Sydney's agent, sent *The Straits Impregnable* to George Robertson, the canny Scottish managing director of publishing company Angus & Robertson. Harry warned Sydney that getting a decision to publish could take some time.

Meanwhile, Sydney was finding himself attracted to one of Elsie Champion's library assistants, the attractive and vivacious Evelyn Cooke, who emphasised her raven-dark hair and gypsy good looks by wearing gold earrings and a long flowing skirt. She told Sydney she was a "resting actress" and her passion was for theatre, although she also loved reading. Evelyn's parents, wealthy graziers in the western districts of Victoria, had sent her to boarding school and taken her on several trips to Europe before the war.

Elsie Champion had no children of her own and took a motherly interest in Sydney. She also knew that Evelyn was used to being wined and dined in style, and liked the best of everything. She warned Sydney that Evelyn had expensive tastes, hoping that this would put an end to their relationship. However, the volatile and sexually liberated Evelyn was intrigued by the good-looking war hero-turned-author, and persuaded him to take her to expensive restaurants.

Denied the company of women for so long, Sydney acknowledged that he had become obsessed by Evelyn's "beautiful body and her wildness".[3] But winning her favour came at a price. Sydney had no job and very little capital and was banking on the publication of *The Straits Impregnable*, which, he hoped, would provide him with some income from royalties.

It came as a nasty shock when Harry Champion informed him that Angus & Robertson had rejected his manuscript. Had Sydney known more about the hazards of Australian publishing he would have realised that George Robertson was a very cautious publisher. Robertson duly returned the manuscript with a standard rejection slip, but added that the author's handling of dialogue and descriptive passages were good. Angus & Robertson would be interested in commissioning an adventure novel by Sydney de Loghe: it was to be set in the outback and had to include some love scenes.

By now Harry Champion and Sydney had become good friends. Harry knew Sydney had just received a small sum from the sale of his stock, and he suggested that if Sydney put up half the printing costs, Harry's literary agency, the Australasian Authors' Agency, would pay the balance.

Sydney was still a serving soldier, and thus subject to Army regulations and the War Precautions Act. But Harry reassured him that publishing *The Straits*

Impregnable as a novel, rather than a war memoir, meant the military censor would not be interested in his story. Sydney trusted Harry's judgement. He slept on the proposal, and next day wrote out a cheque for half the printing costs. When he was off duty, Sydney and Harry edited the typescript together at Champion's book-strewn office, in order to save money.

In July 1916 the first edition of *The Straits Impregnable* was published in Melbourne. *The Lone Hand* reviewed it favourably, praising the quality of Sydney's writing and commenting on the author's excellent use of dialogue. Since Harry Champion had only printed 2000 copies, the book soon sold out. The bookshops wanted more copies, so Harry made preparations for the publication of a second edition.

Being unfit for further combat, Sydney was discharged from the Army on 24 August 1916. The specialists thought it could be one or two years before he would regain full use of his legs. They were convinced he would be cured one day, so Sydney was told he was not eligible for a disability pension. As there were no unemployment benefits at that time, Sydney had to live as best he could on his meagre financial reserves.[4]

On top of this misfortune Sydney received another blow: a black-edged card was delivered to him, announcing the death of Elsie Blair.

After Sydney was discharged from the Army he went to stay with the McGregors, Arthur le Paturel's cousins. After staying there for a few weeks he found inexpensive rooms to rent in the attic of Batman House in William Street, Melbourne. He intended to get on with plotting his second book, hoping to get a contract and an advance from Angus & Robertson.

The attic rooms were cheap because they had no access by lift, no heating, a chipped porcelain bath and a gas geyser, but it was all a destitute author could afford. Although the place was scarcely the setting for a romantic love affair, Sydney invited Evelyn to share his cramped accommodation. Not surprisingly, this caused problems in their relationship; Evelyn, having been spoiled by wealthy parents, continued to demand to be taken out to expensive restaurants, something Sydney could ill afford. He still found her physically exciting, but soon realised that she was shallow, "selfish and hard".[5] Sydney's autobiography and letters to his brother are very frank about the difficulties of their turbulent relationship. Whenever they were together for any length of time they quarrelled; at times Evelyn would storm out and return to her parents' luxurious home in the western districts. It became clear that their relationship was destined to fail.

However, their separations were usually brief. Evelyn would arrange a rendezvous and they would fall into bed and make passionate love again. Then the rows and jealousies erupted again and they would break up once more.

With Evelyn around, Sydney found it hard to concentrate on writing his novel. Nevertheless, Angus & Robertson liked the synopsis he sent them and gave him a contract and a small advance.

★ ★ ★

Intent on seeing his brother, Sydney travelled north by coastal steamer and made his way overland to Mt Cuthbert copper mine, near Mt Isa. He found Charlie, his wife, May, and their little boy, Alasdair, living under the harshest of conditions in a galvanised-iron shed. Sydney moved into another tin shed, beside his brother's, and got on with writing his novel, with no interruptions from Evelyn or anyone else. Inspired by the huge pelicans he saw gliding in to land on a nearby pool, Sydney called his first "real" novel *Pelican Pool*.

In the back of his mind Sydney had a small but comforting hope that while he was away from Melbourne, Evelyn might find another lover and end their turbulent relationship without either of them being hurt.

Back in Melbourne, Harry read *Pelican Pool* but thought it was not nearly as good as *The Straits Impregnable*. Nevertheless, he forwarded the manuscript to Angus & Robertson.

To Sydney's relief, Elsie told him that Evelyn had become involved with a wealthy businessman in what seemed a very serious relationship. Since Sydney was now alone in his stuffy little attic room, Elsie and Harry Champion often invited him to dine at their South Yarra home. In their sitting room, lined with books from floor to ceiling, they spent enjoyable evenings drinking wine and discussing books. Both Harry and Elsie were fond of Sydney and knew that life as a professional author in Australia was very hard. They advised him, once the war was over, to go to London, the centre of publishing, and make it his base.

★　★　★

261

Sydney felt that since his life had been spared at Gallipoli he should try to give something back to those who had been psychologically damaged by war. With this aim in mind he started to work as a volunteer with shell-shocked men at Melbourne's Pelman Institute of Memory Recovery. He became interested in the mental processes that led to war neurosis (as post-traumatic stress and battle fatigue were then called). He read everything he could on the topic, including a book by Sigmund Freud. Freud's theories on the psychological origins of dreams interested Sydney, who was still battling with his own nightmares and sleeping problems.[6]

One day, as Sydney limped along Collins Street, he was hailed by Colonel Johnston. Sydney had greatly admired Johnston as his commander and was pleased to see the colonel, but was concerned that he might be annoyed at being portrayed in *The Straits Impregnable*. To his relief, Colonel Johnston said how much he had enjoyed Sydney's book on Gallipoli, which he thought a very realistic account of what the men had endured on the peninsula. However, he felt that Sydney "had been a little hard on poor Lieutenant Goodwin [Sands]".[7]

Colonel Johnston told Sydney he had prolonged his stay in Melbourne, as his wife had been killed in a riding accident, but he was about to rejoin the remains of his shattered brigade in northern France. The colonel wished Sydney good luck with his book and hoped his stiff leg would soon be better. They shook hands and said goodbye . . . and never met again.[8]

Meanwhile, Harry Champion was busy correcting and checking the proofs of the second edition of *The*

Straits Impregnable before sending them to the printer. Once again he asked Sydney to contribute to the printing costs. Harry decided that since the censor had raised no objections to Sydney de Loghe's alleged "war novel", it was now time to confess that the events related in the book were true.

The Champions and their group of friends, which included Vida Goldstein, lawyer Maurice Blackburn and his wife, Doris, were distressed by the soaring death toll on the Western Front. They had read that the average life expectancy of a young man in the trenches in France was only four weeks. They resented the fact that Prime Minister Billy Hughes insisted that it was Australia's duty to provide men for the Imperial government and continued to press for conscription.[9] Harry Champion hoped that publishing Sydney's narrative as fact rather than fiction might help end the deadlocked trench warfare in France.

The second edition of *The Straits Impregnable* appeared in time for Christmas 1916, complete with the preliminary note: "*This book, written in Australia, Egypt and Gallipoli, is true.*"

However, admitting that *The Straits Impregnable* was factual and never submitting it for censorship was a serious error. Even though Sydney was no longer a serving soldier, the censorship rules had been broken. Unwittingly, Harry Champion had given the military censor the necessary evidence to have the second edition withdrawn under the War Precautions Act.

Some copies of the second edition of *The Straits Impregnable* had already been sold by the time the book had to be withdrawn, which was carried out with the minimum of fuss so as not to jeopardise the publication of *Pelican Pool*.

In order to avoid prosecution, Sydney agreed to write a series of newspaper articles about the German threat to Britain, urging British-born Australians to enlist; Harry would publish them in pamphlet form at a later date.[10]

Sydney noted with annoyance that copies of *The Straits Impregnable* were changing hands under the counter in Melbourne's second-hand bookshops at four times the original price.[11] Over and over again he heard from booksellers that his book was the best account published of the Gallipoli campaign — its sincerity, humour and powerful irony made it an important account of the Australians there.

In the meantime, Miles Franklin had sold the British rights to *The Straits Impregnable* to the London publisher John Murray. In July 1917, shortly after thousands more young men had been slaughtered like animals at the first battle of Passchendaele, the British edition of Sydney's book on Gallipoli appeared.

Australian censors had managed to withhold the truth about Gallipoli because it was so remote. "Embedded" journalists (most of whom had been staying on Imbros Island) wrote whatever the censor's office told them to or had their copy rewritten. British censorship was not as fierce.

However, the conflict on the Western Front was more accessible than the Gallipoli Peninsula, as it could be reached by train from Paris. Independent journalists and photographers saw the horrors of Passchendaele and the Somme for themselves and were shocked. Two outstanding Australian war photographers, Frank Hurley and Hubert Wilkins, took memorable images of the grim conditions under which the Anzacs fought in France. When these photographs appeared in the press, the public was also shocked.

The German Army used mustard gas for the first time on 20 September 1917. From then on the war lost any semblance of glory; photographs of blinded men holding each other's shoulders as they shuffled back to casualty clearing stations sparked public outrage.

Lieutenant Siegfried Sassoon, decorated with a Military Cross for valour, wrote a letter to *The Times* declaring that the war was being prolonged for the benefit of war profiteers and should immediately be stopped by negotiations between the two sides.

The Army threatened Sassoon with a court-martial. His friend Robert Graves urged him to claim that he was suffering from war fatigue and seek treatment in a military hospital.

At this juncture, Harry Champion introduced Sydney to the Melbourne journalist Joice NanKivell, who had given a favourable review of *The Straits Impregnable* in a Melbourne paper.

Joice NanKivell had come to Harry Champion's offices to deliver the manuscript of her second book, *The Solitary Pedestrian*, which Champion had undertaken to publish. The book was intended as a tribute to Joice's younger brother, Geoff NanKivell, who had been killed in northern France.

Joice joined Harry and Sydney for their regular sandwich lunch. Sydney took a liking to Joice's keen intelligence, her warmth and her sense of humour. Like Sydney, she had spent a long time on a struggling Gippsland sheep property. With her short blonde hair and long slim legs, Joice was pleasantly attractive rather than an outstanding beauty like Laura le Paturel or Evelyn Cooke. But by that time Sydney was wary of beautiful women.

Sydney and Joice met again at parties at Harry and Elsie Champion's house and discovered that they had a great deal in common. They both loved the act of writing; both had had problems with their fathers and adored their mothers. Like Sydney's family, Joice's had seen better days. Her father had been declared bankrupt and lost his home and livelihood on a Queensland cane plantation. Joice had grown up in rural poverty on a sheep farm before leaving to work in Melbourne. She yearned to write books and travel overseas.[12] Both of them could read classical Greek and longed to visit Greece.

Elsie Champion was convinced that Joice and Sydney were ideally suited. She sang Joice's praises: Joice was talented, clever, strong-minded and resourceful, she said. But after his disastrous relationships with Laura and Evelyn, Sydney was initially not keen to become emotionally involved with a woman again. Besides, he planned to sail to Ireland, travel to England and try his luck at writing in London. He was going to try to find a suitable topic for a second book for John Murray, who had indicated that he was interested in another non-fiction work from Sydney.

Sydney had arranged to leave Port Melbourne on an old wool clipper, crewed by a team of volunteers. He knew it would be a dangerous journey. The ship, bound for the port of Queenstown (the old name for Covh) near Cork, would sail around Cape Horn, known as the "mariners' graveyard". They intended to start the voyage shortly after peace was declared.

Joice confided in Elsie that she was very attracted to Sydney, and that although he seemed to like her, he never made the slightest advance. Elsie explained that Sydney's experiences with Evelyn had made him cautious about women and his precarious financial position stopped him from even thinking about marriage.

The withdrawal of *The Straits Impregnable* from the market and the pulping of the remaining copies were a big financial setback for Sydney (and for Harry Champion, who went bankrupt a few years later). Sydney's novel *Pelican Pool* had not lived up to expectations, and sales would barely cover the publisher's advance. Sydney's hope of making money from writing lay with the British edition of *The Straits Impregnable*, which was selling well in London.

Finally, with the participation of the Americans, the tide of the war was turning. By the middle of 1918, the German populace was desperately short of food and extreme hunger drove them to revolt. There was hope that the Allies might win after all.

Eventually the Kaiser abdicated and fled to neutral Holland. A ceasefire was arranged, to be signed at 11a.m. on 11 November 1918, but even in the war's last hours hundreds of young men died. During the war, millions had been killed and empires had collapsed. The public was assured that this had been the "war to end all wars", which in hindsight has proven to be a ludicrous assertion.

In January 1919 the Champions gave a party, which may have had something to do with celebrating Sydney's thirtieth birthday. Perhaps it was the champagne, but Sydney told Joice he loved her and asked her to marry him before he sailed to Ireland in a few weeks' time.

Joice was convinced Sydney was the right man for her, so she had no hesitation in accepting his proposal and starting a new life with him. She did not see his departure to Ireland as an impediment, because she was planning to go overseas herself in the near future, and knew that they would meet up in London. Her mother, Edith Lawson, was born in England, and Joice had always wanted to go there. She had grown up hearing her mother's stories of life in Britain and had often been invited to stay with her English relatives.

However, organising a wedding at such short notice was a considerable problem. As Joice had expected, her father was furious when she asked him for money for their wedding. He flatly refused to give her away or attend the wedding. George NanKivell regarded writing as a foolish way to make a living. He told his daughter he had hoped she would find a man of substance to marry — not a penniless author who had written a banned book and a failed novel. But Joice was convinced she could get work as a freelance journalist, and she believed in Sydney as a writer; he surely could find another project. After all, John Murray had promised to consider a suitable story for another book by Sydney de Loghe.

Joice's father was so angry he forbade his wife to attend the wedding ceremony, claiming the marriage was bound to be a disaster and they should have nothing to do with it.

The Lochs' wedding took place at the Scots Presbyterian Church on Royal Parade, Melbourne, on 22 February 1919.[13] Since Joice's mother was not allowed to attend and the newlyweds needed what little money they had to support them in their first weeks in London, they decided it would be a totally private ceremony. Apart from the clergyman, Harry and Elsie Champion were the only two guests, and acted as witnesses.

A few days after the wedding Sydney's clipper left Port Melbourne for Queenstown. His experiences during the nightmare journey round Cape Horn provided background material for another book. He began to write it on board ship but did not finish it until 1925. The book would be published in London a year later.[14]

Shortly after Sydney's departure, the new Mrs Loch travelled to England on a troopship. After landing in

London she stayed in the Lyceum Club in Piccadilly, awaiting Sydney's arrival. When she heard the news that Sydney's ship was missing in a storm, Joice feared that she was a widow before she had been a wife.

Eventually Sydney arrived in London unscathed, but by that time Joice had left the Lyceum Club and was staying with cousins in the country. Without enough money to pay for expensive London hotels, Sydney went to visit his mother, who was overjoyed to see her son after so many years.

Sydney's mother told him that Laura and Frederick had quarrelled bitterly and refused to speak to each other, and that Laura had moved to Scotland. At first his mother refused to tell Sydney why, but then she burst into tears and told him the terrible thing he already knew. Laura, who had always been so kind to his mother, had been Frederick's secret lover for years and was now pregnant with his child.

Sydney was so angry he refused to speak to his father. He borrowed a car and drove to Scotland to see Laura. The image he had carried in his heart all these years was shattered. Laura was desperately unhappy — the *chagrins d'amour* she had sung about at that birthday party had arrived with a vengeance.

Laura confessed her sad story to Sydney. She told Sydney that she planned to have the baby adopted, aware that being a single mother meant that "polite society" would ostracise her.

Saddened by Laura's predicament, Sydney returned to London. Little did he know that six months later Laura would die in childbirth and he and his brother

Eric would be standing beside her grave. Laura's little boy was adopted by the childless lady doctor who had delivered him.[15]

Initially Sydney feared that, since London was full of unemployed returned soldiers, he would never find a job. But his worries were unfounded. He soon found employment at London's Pelman Institute, working once again with shell-shocked soldiers. Joice became a freelance journalist, and after a long search the Lochs managed to find a rental apartment they could afford. George NanKivell's gloomy predictions about Joice and Sydney's marriage proved unfulfilled, as they were very happy together.

Sir John Murray kept his promise and commissioned the Lochs to write a book together on the Anglo- Irish war.

On 21 January 1919 Sinn Fein had declared Ireland independent, and its military wing, the IRA, began attacking British targets. Sydney's mother and Joice's relatives warned them about the potential danger in writing a book about the Anglo-Irish war and urged them not to go to Dublin. But Sydney and Joice did not heed their warnings, and from that time onwards they would never be far away from turbulence and danger.

Installed in a lodging house in Dublin, which unbeknown to them was used as an IRA safe house, the Lochs did their best to write an even-handed book on the situation in Ireland. The British thought Sydney was spying for the Irish and briefly imprisoned him, while the IRA regarded Sydney as a double agent.

When the situation in Ireland became too dangerous for them, the Lochs returned to London. But once their book on the Irish Troubles — titled *Ireland in Travail* — was published, London was not safe for them either, so they were advised to get as far away as possible.

By now the Russian Imperial family was dead. The Bolsheviks under Lenin sent Russian troops to invade eastern Poland where they wreaked vengeance on devout Polish Catholic peasants who refused to embrace Marxism. Lenin ordered his troops to burn Polish villages and destroy their crops, to rape Polish women and kill Polish men. Once again clever spin doctoring was used to present the Russian side of the story, while the truth remained hidden. The War Victims' Relief arm of the Quakers (or the Society of Friends) found it hard to raise money for starving Poles, while most donations went to Lenin's brave new Socialist-Marxist experiment.

Thousands of Polish war victims would have starved to death had it not been for Friends' War Relief. The starving Poles faced a harsh winter in sub-zero temperatures without food or housing. In order to write a book about the "forgotten" Russo-Polish war the Lochs became unpaid volunteer aid workers with the Society of Friends on the Polish-Russian frontier.[16]

In Poland Sydney set up imaginative aid schemes to rebuild entire Polish villages and, using his knowledge of farming methods, he established and ran a Farm School for orphaned boys. Joice worked in medical centres where she deloused war victims and learned basic medical practices.

After working in Poland the Lochs were asked to volunteer to help Greek victims of Turkish ethnic cleansing. At the end of World War I, Australia's old enemy the Ottoman Empire disintegrated and the Sultan abdicated. On 15 May 1919, Greece, under President Venizelos, landed a Greek army in Turkey at the Hellenic settlement of Smyrna (today's Izmir) to enforce a Greek claim to the area. Kemal Ataturk, the officer who had rallied the Turks at Gallipoli, formed a national government and his army slaughtered most of the Greek troops sent to Smyrna and hundreds of thousands of Greek Orthodox civilians — who had lived in Turkey for generations — in a vicious campaign of ethnic cleansing. Subsequently the League of Nations undertook an exchange of Turkish residents in Greece with the remaining Greeks residing in Turkey.

The Quakers called for more volunteers to work with these Greek Orthodox refugees, who came from all over Asia Minor as well as Turkey and numbered well over one and a half million.

Sydney and Joice had always dreamed of visiting Greece and, though tired by their efforts in Poland (where Joice had lost a much-wanted baby), they unselfishly volunteered once more to work in a refugee camp, this time on the campus of the American Farm School, near Thessaloniki. They worked there until all the Greek refugees had been re-housed.

By that time Sydney had received a contract to write a history of the Mount Athos peninsula near

273

Thessaloniki, which is famous for its twenty Orthodox monasteries. He and Joice set up house in an ancient stone tower in the refugee village Ouranoupolis, in the shadow of Athos, the Holy Mountain. The Lochs set about improving conditions for the refugee villagers, who found themselves without a proper water supply or any form of medical assistance. Sydney and Joice provided medicine and bandages and raised funds to install an unpolluted water supply system, for which work they were awarded medals by the Greek government. Gradually life improved for the villagers.

In 1927 the Lochs sailed from the port of Ouranoupolis to the isle of Skyros aboard a yacht owned by Greek friends. On Skyros they went to see the grave of Rupert Brooke (1887–1915), the great English poet who had romanticised war. Ironically he had died from blood poisoning, caused by a mosquito bite he had received while on a hospital ship anchored in Tres Boukris Bay. A team of Australians had carried his corpse up to an olive grove overlooking the sea and buried him there.

Sydney and Joice and their friends climbed the long path from the bay up the side of the mountain to see the grave of the poet on which was inscribed his most famous poem "The Soldier".

If I should die, think only this of me,
That there's some corner of a foreign field
That is forever England.

Sydney read the poem aloud and observed that, had Rupert Brooke actually lived long enough to fight at Gallipoli, his war poems would not have been so romantic.

From the island of Skyros they sailed to the province of Canakkale in Turkey on the Dardanelles Straits. They landed on the narrow strip of beach at Anzac Cove. Joice was amazed to see how Sydney and the rest of the Anzacs had lived — on a mountainside honeycombed with man-made caves.

By that time the Australian War Graves Commission had installed a resident guardian there. The original wooden crosses erected by the Anzacs had rotted away or been used for firewood by the local peasants. Now the crosses were being replaced by small stone monuments, quarried locally. Sydney visited the graves of many of his comrades-in-arms. He knew how lucky he was to be alive and more than ever he felt the need — and a responsibility — to use his life to help victims of war.

By 1929 military censorship concerning World War I had become a thing of the past. Veterans of the bloodiest conflict in history felt they must speak out against war and the public was eager to read what they revealed. That year two autobiographical novels about the horrors of the Western Front became best-sellers. Erich Maria Remarque's novel *All Quiet on the Western Front* and Robert Graves's *Goodbye to All That* both carried messages about the futility and the brutality of war. Both books sold very well. *Goodbye to All That* paid Robert Graves enough money to establish himself in a house at Deya on the island of Mallorca.

Like Sydney Loch, Robert Graves had written *Goodbye to All That* in an attempt to get the horrors of war out of his system. Sydney thought Graves's autobiographical book was excellent in most respects, but having talked to many veterans of the Western Front did not agree with Graves's statement that the Australians had treated their prisoners shamefully: certainly he had not seen them do so with Turkish prisoners at Gallipoli.

Sydney felt there was "far too much self pity" and sensationalism in Remarque's *All Quiet on the Western Front*. In the prologue to a revised version of his own Gallipoli experiences, which was to be fictionalised, under a new title with a romance incorporated, he wrote that self pity had been totally "foreign to the Anzac spirit".[17] His publishers decided they preferred the original book, so this version was never published.

The success of these accounts of the horrors, immorality and sheer futility of war did, however, cause John Murray's publishing house to plan an updated (fourth) edition of *The Straits Impregnable* under the pen name of Sydney de Loghe. By now there was a *Zeitgeist*, or spirit of the times, that matched the feelings of Sydney and Harry Champion — that there must be a more intelligent way of settling disputes than slaughtering almost an entire generation of young men.

Murray's contacted Sydney, who was now working in Greece, about the plan and suggested he cut parts of

The Straits Impregnable and add a chapter relating to his work with refugees after the Russian-Polish war and during the Greek-Turkish war.

The project was delayed as Sydney was working as a teacher at the American Farm School for war orphans as well as writing a history of Mount Athos and its twenty Orthodox monasteries for Lutterworth Press. He was also finishing a play about the struggles of the Black and Tans and Sinn Fein in Ireland.[18]

Then Hitler invaded Poland and once more the Lochs became involved in aid work with Polish war victims.

During World War II, while running a refugee centre in Bucharest with the help of the British War Office, Sydney planned and executed a spectacular coup to snatch over 1,000 Jews and Poles from death just before the Nazis invaded Romania. He risked his life to lead a group of Polish refugees via Constantinople to Cyprus and to British-mandated Palestine. There he and Joice ran two adjoining camps for Polish refugees until the end of the war.

After World War II, Sydney acted as temporary Head of the Farm School at Thessaloniki and re-established the school, whose buildings had been sacked by the invading Germans. He and Joice also helped rebuild the shattered village of Ouranoupolis and then Sydney returned to teaching boys at the American Farm School.[19]

After losing her much-wanted baby in Poland, Joice never got pregnant again, so Sydney was thrilled when a Greek couple by the name of Marangou asked him to act as godfather to their daughter who would be named after him. Sydney Loch paid for her education at the Farm School and at a French convent in Thessaloniki. To get the money for his beloved goddaughter's education as a nurse in London he had to sell his most valuable possession: an old Army jeep. Today, a mature woman living in England, Sydney's goddaughter, Sydney White, still remembers him with fondness and gratitude.

Sydney Loch died in his tower home in the village of Ouranoupolis during the winter in 1954. Typically, he had insisted on going out into the snow to rescue a wounded pelican; a short time later he died. A period of living in a war zone on a very restricted diet, combined with severe typhoid fever, had no doubt contributed to a weakening heart.

Sydney was buried in the grounds of the American Farm School where he had taught for so many years. The funeral address praised his "outstanding qualities of integrity, impartiality and self-discipline ... combined with a sympathetic understanding of the plight of the victims of war".[20]

Gallipoli had indeed changed Sydney Loch from a soldier to a humanitarian and he fulfilled the promise he made on his second visit to Gallipoli: to dedicate the rest of his life to helping the victims of war.

Twenty-eight years later, in 1982, Joice Loch died at the age of ninety-five. She was buried among olive groves overlooking the sea at Ouranoupolis. Shortly after Joice died, Sydney's body was moved from the

American Farm School and reburied in a joint grave with his wife.

Chiselled in the memorial tablet on Sydney Loch's grave is a poem he wrote in his youth:

Let me take wing as swallows wing
To where summer dwells,
Striking the clouds as autumn's sting
On the meadow falls
My fleshy home with gladness leave,
And to thee return,
Cleaving to thee as swallows cleave
To where summers burn.
Let me approach to thee, so pass
On as swallows speed,
That skim a last time o'er the grass
Of the watered mead.
This ailing flesh my green fields are
Where autumn runs,
And I arriving from afar
Towards new suns.

On 6 July 2006 a small museum honouring the work of Joice and Sydney Loch was opened in their former tower home at Ouranoupolis where one of the projects the Lochs had supported was the establishment of a rug-making industry by the refugees. One of the "Pirgos rugs", found in Australia, was donated to the museum by Mr Paul Tighe, Australian Ambassador to Greece.

Also displayed in the museum are busts of Sydney and Joice, which were donated by the American Farm School at Thessaloniki.

ENDNOTES

Introduction

1. No publisher is given for the Rules for Censors. A copy is held in the library of the Australian War Memorial.

2. Information about the forced withdrawal from sale of the second edition of *The Straits Impregnable* was referred to in one of the letters Sydney Loch had sent to his brother Charles, who was working in central Queensland at the time. After Charles's death Sydney's letters were passed on to Charles's son, Iain Loch, who related the contents of the relevant letter to us. The letter describes Sydney's anguish over the withdrawal of the second edition of *The Straits Impregnable* and the financial loss incurred. Sydney was not allowed to publicise any reference to the withdrawal.

3. Sydney de Loghe (Loch), *One Crowded Hour, a Call to Arms*, Australasian Author's Agency, Melbourne, 1918.

4. Letter, Miles Franklin to Elsie Goldstein, 21 October 1916, Private collection.

5. Noel Carthew, *Voices from the Trenches: Letters to Home*, New Holland, Sydney, 2002, page 30 refers to Lieutenant Charles Carthew's dislike of censoring personal letters written by his soldiers.

6. General Sir Ian Hamilton was in his sixties at the time of the Gallipoli campaign.

7. "Spin doctors" invented tales of German soldiers raping Belgian nuns to whip up rage in the first days of World War I. In the same way, exaggerated stories were released to newspapers all over the "free" world during wars in Korea and Vietnam. American Government spin doctors invented tales about ailing Kuwaiti babies snatched by Iraqi troops from incubators and left to die to incite American feeling against Saddam Hussein. See John R. MacArthur, *Second Front: Censorship and Propaganda in the Gulf War*, University of California Press, Berkeley CA, 2004.

8. Australians were kept in the dark about the extent of the disaster at Gallipoli. F. and E. Brenchley, in *Myth Maker: Ellis Ashmead-Bartlett, The Englishman Who Sparked Australia's Gallipoli Legend*, John Wiley, Brisbane, 2005, claim that notwithstanding the substantial death toll on the first day and night at Anzac Cove, the Australian Government released no casualty figures until 2 May 1915, when they listed a mere 18 Australians dead and 37 wounded.

9. See Philip Knightley, *The First Casualty — From the Crimea to Vietnam, the War Correspondent as Hero, Propagandist and Myth Maker*, Harcourt

Brace Jovanovich, New York and London, 1975, pp 100–103.

10. Brenchley, *Myth Maker: Ellis Ashmead-Bartlett*.

11. Les Carlyon, *Gallipoli*, Macmillan, Sydney, 2002, p 495.

12. Keith Murdoch's Gallipoli letter is archived in the National Library of Australia.

13. Papers relating to Ashmead-Bartlett's lecture tour of Australia, MP 390/8 and B/C 3578435, Diaries 1915/16, National Archives of Australia. Ashmead-Bartlett's original letter is printed in full in Brenchley, *Myth Maker: Ellis Ashmead-Bartlett*.

Prologue

1. Sydney Loch, unpublished autobiography, Sydney Loch papers, Manuscript Collection, National Library of Australia, Canberra, MS 2404; details confirmed by other members of the Loch family.

2. From the Loch papers owned by Martha Handschin and sighted by Iain Loch.

3. Sydney Loch, unpublished autobiography, Sydney Loch papers.

4. The tales of the rape of the Belgian nuns were largely anti-German propaganda used by the British and French to persuade young Catholic men to enlist and fight the German army.

5. In *The Straits Impregnable* Sydney did not mention that the McGregors had spoken to Colonel Johnston, who appears in *The Straits Impregnable* as "Colonel Jackson".

The Straits Impregnable

1. Sydney mentions in a letter to his brother that he took a framed photograph of Laura with him to Australia, but there is no indication as to whether he took it with him when he went to war.

2. Elsie Blair, daughter of the manager of Kirndean Station, had made the long journey to Broadmeadows to bring Sydney several pairs of warm socks and a khaki balaclava she had knitted herself. Sydney Loch omitted this incident with Elsie Blair in *The Straits Impregnable*, but it is recorded in his unpublished papers, held in the Manuscript Department of the National Library of Australia.

3. In this context pickets are men who guard horses or tether horses to pegs in the ground.

4. Sydney embarked on HMAT *Shropshire*, which he referred to as the SS *Blankshire* in *The Straits Impregnable*, since naming Australian troopships in war time was an offence.

5. Later Sydney Loch learned that the *Uranus* had struck them astern and again amidships; after the collision she steamed away into the dark.

6. Initially there were no latrines in the area designated at Mena Camp for Australian and New Zealand troops. Colonel Neville Howse, as senior Australian medical officer, insisted latrines be built as soon as possible for health reasons.

7. Mena House had been built in 1869 as a hunting lodge for the Egyptian Royal Family and later became a hotel. Subsequently, the building was a

British hospital and later an Australian Army hospital.

8. A *gharri* is a type of carriage drawn by one or two horses.

9. The "Wazir" or "Wozzer" was the brothel district of Cairo. Riots took place here during which New Zealand and Australian troops burned down a brothel, claiming it had overcharged for drinks and its inmates had infected some men with syphilis. The troops had received warnings from medical officers regarding the dangers of syphilis, but so many cases of venereal disease were recorded that Major-General Bridges issued a warning to the troops of the dangers of consorting with "public women".

10. These were planted originally by Napoleon on his Egyptian campaign so that his wife, Josephine, might view the Pyramids in comfort.

11. The *Hindoo* is likely to have been a pseudonym for HMAT *Karroo*, which was used as a troopship to Gallipoli and for carrying the wounded back to Egypt.

12. Mudros (now Mudhros on the island of Lemnos) is one of the finest natural harbours in the Aegean. The Allies initially intended to land their entire expeditionary force there so that the horses could recuperate from the sea voyage. But they failed to take into account that Lemnos, with its low rainfall, did not have enough fresh water for 3,000 men and their horses. After heated discussion between the British and Australian commanding

officers, only one battalion was billeted ashore; the rest, including Sydney Loch's brigade, had to remain on board ship in Mudros Harbour. They were not told why this was necessary.

13. It must have been clear to Colonel Jackson (Johnston) that Sydney was an educated and intelligent young man; this is probably why he promoted him. Sydney's unpublished autobiography relates that shortly before being invalided back to Alexandria he was interviewed to be promoted to an officer, and passed the interview. Sydney modestly attributed his promotion to so many officers being killed.

14. Very few Australian horses were landed at Gallipoli, as it was too difficult to use them in the rugged area where the Anzacs landed. As the British had landed on more level terrain, they took their horses ashore.

15. Sappers are soldiers who make fortifications or dig trenches that are known as "saps".

16. The Anzacs were almost a mile (1.6km) north of where they should have landed. The correct spot had much easier terrain for an attack. Various reasons have been advanced for this.

17. By the time Sydney Loch's brigade arrived at Anzac Cove in the afternoon of 25 April, many of the dead had been buried, which meant that initially Sydney was unaware of how many had died earlier that day, but he saw large numbers of wounded on the beach.

18. Sydney Loch often uses the word "funk-hole"

instead of "dugout". Literally, a funk-hole is a refuge from "something feared" or a bolthole from danger.

19. There is no indication as to whether the guns actually went back, but this seems unlikely, as additional guns arrived at Anzac Cove on the following day.

20. Two of Birdwood's divisional commanders were keen to withdraw. Birdwood reluctantly passed on their recommendations to the Commander-in-Chief, Sir Ian Hamilton, but Sydney Loch is unlikely to have known this at the time. See Alan Moorehead, *Gallipoli*, Hamish Hamilton, 1956; and Cyril Pearl, *Anzac Newsreel: A Picture History of Gallipoli*, Ure Smith, Sydney, 1963.

21. Within days over 20,000 Australian troops and 10,000 New Zealanders occupied a semi-circle of land less than one mile (1.6km) in depth and one and a half miles (2.5km) in length.

22. The men who were "stunned" by continuous shelling were in fact shell-shocked (ie, suffering from war neurosis), but at the time little was known about that condition (see also endnote 29).

23. The hospital ships stayed several miles from the shore to keep out of range of the Turkish guns, so the wounded had to be ferried out to them by barges and pinnaces.

24. The bay to which Sydney refers is now known as Anzac Cove.

25. Sir Ian Hamilton issued the order to "Dig, dig, dig"; after that the Australian soldiers started

digging in earnest and soon acquired the name "diggers".

26. A high explosive named because it was first tested at Lydd in Kent.

27. A howitzer is a short-barrelled cannon, used for firing shells in a steep arc to reach troops in trenches and behind cover.

28. Private John Kirkpatrick Simpson, 3rd Field Ambulance, AIF, would become an Anzac legend for bravery and compassion as "the man with the donkey". He was said to be using several runaway donkeys to bring down the wounded. On 19 May 1915 Simpson (the name under which he had enlisted) was shot through the heart by a Turkish sniper.

29. The man referred to was clearly shell-shocked. During World War I men suffering these symptoms were often regarded as cowards and treated accordingly. Pioneering research into shell-shock (war neurosis) was carried out at Craiglockhart Hospital for Officers near Edinburgh, and the famous soldier poets Siegfried Sassoon and Wilfred Owen, both suffering from shell-shock, were treated there by Dr W. H. Rivers. Sydney Loch's encounters with sufferers of shell-shock in various military hospitals would lead him to read what was known about shell-shock when he worked with brain-damaged war victims in Melbourne and at London's Pelman Institute for Memory Loss when World War I was over.

30. This description clearly indicates that Sydney

Loch at that time regarded himself as more Australian than British.

31. Many of those buried in these small graves would later be moved to the larger Anzac Cemetery, which is still there today.

32. In *The Straits Impregnable* and his unpublished papers Sydney Loch refers to "Lonesome Pine", which later became famous under the name "Lone Pine". We have used the latter name.

33. "General Runner" is a pseudonym for Brigadier-General Harold Walker, who took command of the 1st Division after the death of Major-General Bridges.

34. "General Rivers" is a pseudonym for Major-General Bridges. Likewise, below, "Captain Carrot" is a pseudonym for the war correspondent Charles Bean. In his autobiography Sydney Loch gives Bean his real name. Bean also had red hair, a trait which is mentioned in the entry on him in the *Australian Dictionary of Biography*, vol 7.

35. Sydney Loch may have been told that Bean intended to write an account of Anzac troops on foreign soil. Bean was annoyed that he had to stay on the island of Imbros and was only allowed on the Gallipoli Peninsula twice or three times a week.

36. Quinn's Post was the most dangerous of all the Anzac sites because the Turkish trenches were close. Casualties there were very high. It is where a Turkish bullet severed an artery in the leg of Major-General "Bill" Bridges. On 18 May 1915

Bridges was taken by barge to the hospital ship *Gascon*, but en route he died of gangrene.

37. Harvey Broadbent records in *Gallipoli — The Fatal Shore* (Viking, Melbourne, 2005) that at first permission for a truce was refused. Sydney Loch relates that during the initial discussions it was agreed that the Turks could send a staff officer the following morning to discuss the matter further with General Braithwaite at Birdwood's HQ.

38. Harvey Broadbent records in *Gallipoli — The Fatal Shore* that the Turkish officer was blindfolded and taken on a diversionary route to Birdwood's HQ. The truce took place on 24 May.

39. Anzac Cove, with Turkish guns trained on it, was now seen by the British Admiralty as too dangerous to allow supply ships within range.

40. C. E. W. Bean's *Official History of the War of 1914–1918* makes the same observation.

41. Michael Tyquin, *Gallipoli: The Medical War*, UNSW Press, Sydney, 1993, cites dysentery as "severe inflammation of the colon with stomach pain and acute diarrhoea which can be amoebic or bacillic". Dysentery caused frequent bouts of diarrhoea, often requiring the patient to go to the latrines almost every hour and accompanied by severe bouts of intestinal pain. Little or no toilet paper was provided in the latrines.

42. The Turks called Lone Pine "Kahhsirt" or "The Bloody Ridge", so fierce was the battle fought there. Seven thousand Turks and Australians died at Lone Pine, and for years afterwards whitening

piles of bones could be seen there. However, most of the bones were buried by the time of Sydney's return visit to Gallipoli in 1924.

Epilogue

1. Sydney was perhaps lucky. The *Gascon*, another Australian hospital ship crowded with patients from Lone Pine and Suvla Bay, was advised that it would have to go as far afield as Malta to find beds for the wounded in a British Army hospital. Susanna de Vries, *Heroic Australian Women in War: Astonishing Tales of Bravery from Gallipoli to Kokoda*, HarperCollins, Sydney, 2004.

2. Sydney describes Elsie Blair moving to Brighton and her subsequent death on pp 307–308 of his unpublished autobiography, Sydney Loch Papers, Manuscripts Department, National Library of Australia, Canberra, MS 2040.

3. *Ibid.*

4. *Ibid.* Colonel A. C. Butler, DSO, MB, Ch.B., author of *The Official History of the Australian Army Medical Services*, stated that 181 soldiers received a pension due to the ill effects of dysentery, 56 due to "enteric" or typhoid and 156 due to "polyneuritis". Sydney should have received a pension up to the time of his recovery two years later but did not, and he had twinges of pain for another decade. Unemployment benefits were only introduced to Australia by a Labour Government in World War II.

5. Sydney Loch, unpublished autobiography.
6. Later, in 1927, Sydney visited his brother Eric, who was then studying singing in Vienna. There he interviewed Sigmund Freud on his theories of the interpretation of dreams in therapy. However, Freud's insistence on the importance of the id and the ego and infant sexuality did not impress Sydney. He was struggling to help Greek boys whose fathers had been murdered by the Turks at Smyrna and who had witnessed terrible sights there. He instead took a short course of study in psychology with Dr Albert Adler, which he found helpful in his work with troubled boys.
7. These were Colonel Johnston's own words as recorded in Sydney's unpublished autobiography, Sydney Loch papers.
8. Colonel Johnston rejoined the Anzacs in France and survived. He died during World War II and was buried in Brighton Cemetery, Melbourne. Sydney records that Lieutenant Goodwin (Sands) also stayed in the artillery, was promoted to captain and served in World War II.
9. Patrick Carlyon, *The Story of Gallipoli*, Penguin Books, Melbourne, 2004, pp 149.
10. See the Introduction to this book for details of *One Crowded Hour*, the pamphlet by Sydney Loch.
11. Noted in Sydney Loch, unpublished autobiography.
12. The stories of Sydney and Joice NanKivell Loch are related in detail in Susanna de Vries, *Blue*

Ribbons, Bitter Bread, Tower Books, Sydney, 2004.

13. Joice's biography, *A Fringe of Blue*, was written in her old age after she had suffered a bad fall and subsequent memory loss. The book's cover blurb, which claims that the Lochs married in England, is wrong. The marriage certificate relating to the wedding at the Scots Church in Melbourne is held in Melbourne's Registry of Births, Marriages and Deaths.

14. Sydney de Loghe, *Three Predatory Women*, London, 1926.

15. In his unpublished autobiography, Sydney provides a poignant description of Laura's funeral attended only by himself, Joice and his brothers. Laura's illegitimate son, Sydney's half-brother, was adopted but kept in touch with Sydney and eventually visited him in Ouranoupolis. Additional information about this was received from the late Iain Loch, whose father also attended the funeral, and from Fani Mitropoulou, who learned the story from Joice Loch. Laura's son became a distinguished academic but by family request Sydney's half-brother's name is withheld from this book.

16. Sydney Loch and Joice NanKivell, *The River of a Thousand Ways: Life in War-torn Poland*, was published by Allen and Unwin in London in 1926.

17. Sydney attempted to write a proper novel about his Gallipoli experiences, told from the viewpoint of a former jackeroo named John Irvine with an added love interest. The manuscript titled *Turn'd*

But Not Torn is in the Australian War Memorial library, item no. 1367, but its love scenes were unconvincing and the novel remained unpublished.

18. Sydney's play *Forty-Seven*, based on his experiences with Sinn Fein and his friend, the British agent Algy Garnett, who features in *Blue Ribbons, Bitter Bread* as Major X, was performed in London in February 1930. One of the patrons behind its production was the famous Irish writer George Bernard Shaw. The MS is among the Sydney Loch papers in the Australian National Library in Canberra. Sydney's literary agent, A. W. Peters (now Peters Dunlop), sold film rights to a Hollywood producer in 1937. Sydney intended to use the profits to help the refugee village of Ouranoupolis, but filming was postponed due to the start of World War II, and the film was in fact never made.

19. Sydney Loch's life and achievements, from the time he left Australia, are described in greater detail in *Blue Ribbons, Bitter Bread*.

20. A copy of Sydney Loch's valedictory address was provided by his Greek goddaughter, Sydney Marangou White, who lives partly in England but spends her summers in Greece. She spoke very movingly about her godfather on the ABC's *Foreign Correspondent*, celebrating the opening of the Joice and Sydney Loch Memorial Museum in 2006.

ACKNOWLEDGEMENTS

Special thanks are due to Sydney Loch's Greek goddaughter, Sydney White, for information and photographs of her much-loved godfather.

Special thanks are also due to the late Iain Loch, son of Sydney's brother Charles. Being in possession of letters from Sydney to Charles, Iain Loch could provide valuable information about the withdrawal of the second edition of *The Straits Impregnable*. He also put us in touch with the widow of Sydney's half-brother (the illegitimate son of Sydney's father and his pupil, young heiress Laura le Paturel). Unfortunately, Iain Loch died in hospital in England at the end of 2006, so he did not live long enough to see the completion of the book to which he has contributed important information.

Warmest thanks are extended to Australian-born Georgina Loch Jarvenpaa, another descendant of Charles Loch. She provided a copy of the Loch family crest and several photographs, which we highly valued since most of Sydney's photographs, held in the tower at Ouranoupolis, were destroyed by Communist guerrillas during World War II.

Swiss-born Martha Handschin of Ouranoupolis also provided information and photographs, as did Fani Mitropoulou, the Lochs' former housekeeper. Thanks are also due to Byzantine Museums for allowing us access to Loch papers and artefacts, to Daryl K. Povey and to other private sources (who wish to remain anonymous) for supplying photographic material.

For helping to get this important eye-witness account of Gallipoli back into print, we thank Shona Martyn, Amruta Slee, Mary Rennie and other staff at HarperCollins; our agent, Selwa Anthony; and our assistant at Pirgos Press, Marusia MacCormick. We also wish to thank the librarians and the bookshop manager of the Australian War Memorial in Canberra.

Last but by no means least we wish to thank Dame Elisabeth Murdoch, who, having read the story of Joice NanKivell Loch in *Blue Ribbons, Bitter Bread*, provided funding for further research into the work of the equally remarkable Sydney Loch.

After World War I, and following his marriage to Joice NanKivell, Sydney became a passionate aid worker, who devoted the rest of his life to helping refugees and victims of war. For this reason a proportion of the royalties raised by this book is being donated to World Vision for its water health program, bringing wells and unpolluted water to villages in third-world countries; a program in sympathy with the work of Sydney Loch.

Bomber Boys

Patrick Bishop

The 125,000 men from all over the world who passed through Bomber Command were engaged in a form of warfare that had never been implemented before. Between 1940 and 1945 they flew continuously, stopping only when weather made operations impossible. There was nothing romantic about their struggle. Often barely out of boyhood, they lived on bleak bases, flying at night on long, nerve-wracking missions that often ended in death. In all, 55,000 were killed, counting for nearly one in ten of all the British and Commonwealth war dead.

In this powerful and moving work of history, Patrick Bishop brilliantly captures the character, feelings and motivations of the bomber crews and pays tribute to their heroism and determination. They were among the best of their generation, who were called on to carry out one of the grimmest duties of the Second World War. Bomber Boys brilliantly restores these men to their rightful place in our consciousness.

ISBN 978-0-7531-5675-9 (hb)
ISBN 978-0-7531-5676-6 (pb)

Brothers in War

Michael Walsh

The Beecheys were a close-knit family: eight brothers and five sisters under the loving eye of their mother, Amy. As the First World War raged, the brothers were swept up into its devastating path. Tragedy followed tragedy as, one after another, the Beechey boys fell. It was a family sacrifice almost without parallel, and one that has remained forgotten and unmarked — until now.

Kept in a small brown case handed down by the brothers' youngest sister were hundreds of letters sent home by the boys. Scraps of paper scribbled on whilst in the firing line, heartfelt letters written from a deathbed and exasperated correspondences detailing the absurdities of life in the trenches.

Piecing together the Beechey story, Michael Walsh interweaves these letters with a moving account of the Great War, and its shattering effects at home and on foreign fields, all told through one family who paid the ultimate price.

ISBN 978-0-7531-9422-5 (hb)
ISBN 978-0-7531-9423-2 (pb)

A Woman in Berlin

Anonymous

Begun on the day when Berlin first saw the face of war,
the anonymous author of *A Woman in Berlin* describes
life within the falling city as it was sacked by the
Russian Army. Fending off the boredom and
deprivation of hiding, she records her experiences,
observations and meditations in this stark and vivid
diary. Reports of the bombing, the rationing of food
and the overwhelming terror of death are written in
dispassionate, though determinedly optimistic, prose. It
caused huge controversy when first published in
German in the 1950s. In 2003, over 40 years later it
was republished in Germany to critical acclaim — and
more controversy.

Newly translated into English, this is an astonishing
and deeply affecting account of a woman fighting for
survival amidst the horror and inhumanity of war.

ISBN 978-0-7531-9376-1 (hb)
ISBN 978-0-7531-9377-8 (pb)

My Life as a Spy

Leslie Woodhead

In the spring of 1956, 18-year-old Leslie Woodhead received a summons to serve Her Majesty. National Service signalled the end of boyhood. But it was the beginning of his "life as a spy".

An only child, living above a shop in post-war Halifax, Woodhead grew up with austerity and secrets. But nothing prepared him for the comically bleak RAF training camps he now found himself in, nor the isolated Joint Services School for Linguistics on the east coast of Scotland. Here he was trained by a colourful staff of émigrés, who taught a course of total immersion in Russian for purposes not always clear to their pupils. A posting to an ex-Luftwaffe base in a war-scarred Berlin provided only partial explanations. In the ruins of a city gripped by espionage and paranoia, he discovers adulthood and his vocation as an observer and documenter of people.

ISBN 978-0-7531-9366-2 (hb)
ISBN 978-0-7531-9367-9 (pb)